FROM

CALCUTTA TO THE SNOWY RANGE

FROM

CALCUTTA TO THE SNOWY RANGE

BEING THE NARRATIVE OF A TRIP

THROUGH THE UPPER PROVINCES OF INDIA TO THE HIMALAYAS,

CONTAINING AN ACCOUNT OF

MONGHYR, BENARES, ALLAHABAD, CAWNPORE, LUCKNOW, AGRA, DELHI, AND SIMLA

BY

AN OLD INDIAN

WITH EIGHT COLOURED ILLUSTRATIONS AND A FLAP

GYAN

Published by

GYAN

Gyan Publishing House
5, Ansari Road
Daryaganj, New Delhi-110002
Phone: 011-47034999, 9811692060
E-mail: books@gyanbooks.com

Distribution Network
gyanbooks.com
India, USA, Canada, UK, Australia, France

ISBN : 978-81-212-3413-9 (PB)
First Published, 1866

2nd Impression 2020

Printed at: Gyan Press, Delhi.

The book at your disposal is the edition of an old book originally published long back. The Text quality of this book may not be at par as compared to our other books but many readers approached us to reprint this important book so that it could satiate their hunger. We request all the readers of this book to help us to improve its quality by providing the necessary text of those pages which are not properly visible. Your valuable support in this case will be highly appreciated and acknowledged and our future readers will be benefitted immensely.

FROM

Calcutta to the Snowy Range;

BEING THE NARRATIVE OF A TRIP

THROUGH THE UPPER PROVINCES OF INDIA TO THE HIMALAYAS,

CONTAINING AN ACCOUNT OF

MONGHYR, BENARES, ALLAHABAD, CAWNPORE, LUCKNOW, AGRA, DELHI, AND SIMLA.

BY

AN OLD INDIAN.

With Eight Coloured Illustrations and a Map.

LONDON:
TINSLEY BROTHERS, CATHERINE STREET, STRAND;
CALCUTTA: WYMAN & CO., HARE STREET.
1866.

THE SNOWY RANGE

PREFACE.

THIS Book, containing the record of a Winter Tour through the upper Provinces of India to the Himalayas, is placed before the Public in the hope that the historical interest of the scenes described, and the peculiarity of the method of Indian, as compared with English travel, may secure for it a perusal which will be of profit to the general reader. It has also been thought that such a Work could not but be of special value to those in India contemplating a like journey. The author's experience has been that chance travellers in that country are unable to procure any adequate or trustworthy account of the places of note visited by all who travel along this route.

It has been specially sought, by careful research and inquiry, to furnish reliable information; and I have to tender my best thanks to Major Chamberlain, Messrs. T. C. Fenwick, W. H. Hoff, W. Smyth, and other gentlemen, who have most kindly assisted me in this respect. I have also to acknowledge that I am indebted for several of my illustrations to admirable photographs taken by Messrs. Bourne and Shepherd, reduced by "our own artist," to suit this Work.

F. F. W.

LONDON, *June*, 1866.

CONTENTS.

CHAPTER I.

INTRODUCTORY.

CHAPTER II.

CALCUTTA TO MONGHYR.

CHAPTER III.

BENARES.

CHAPTER IV.

BENARES TO ALLAHABAD.

CHAPTER V.

CAWNPORE TO LUCKNOW.

CHAPTER VI.

LUCKNOW.

CHAPTER VII.

AGRA.

CHAPTER VIII.

AGRA TO DELHI.

CHAPTER IX.

DELHI TO SIMLA.

CHAPTER X.

SIMLA AND THE SNOWY RANGE.

APPENDIX.

LIST OF ILLUSTRATIONS.

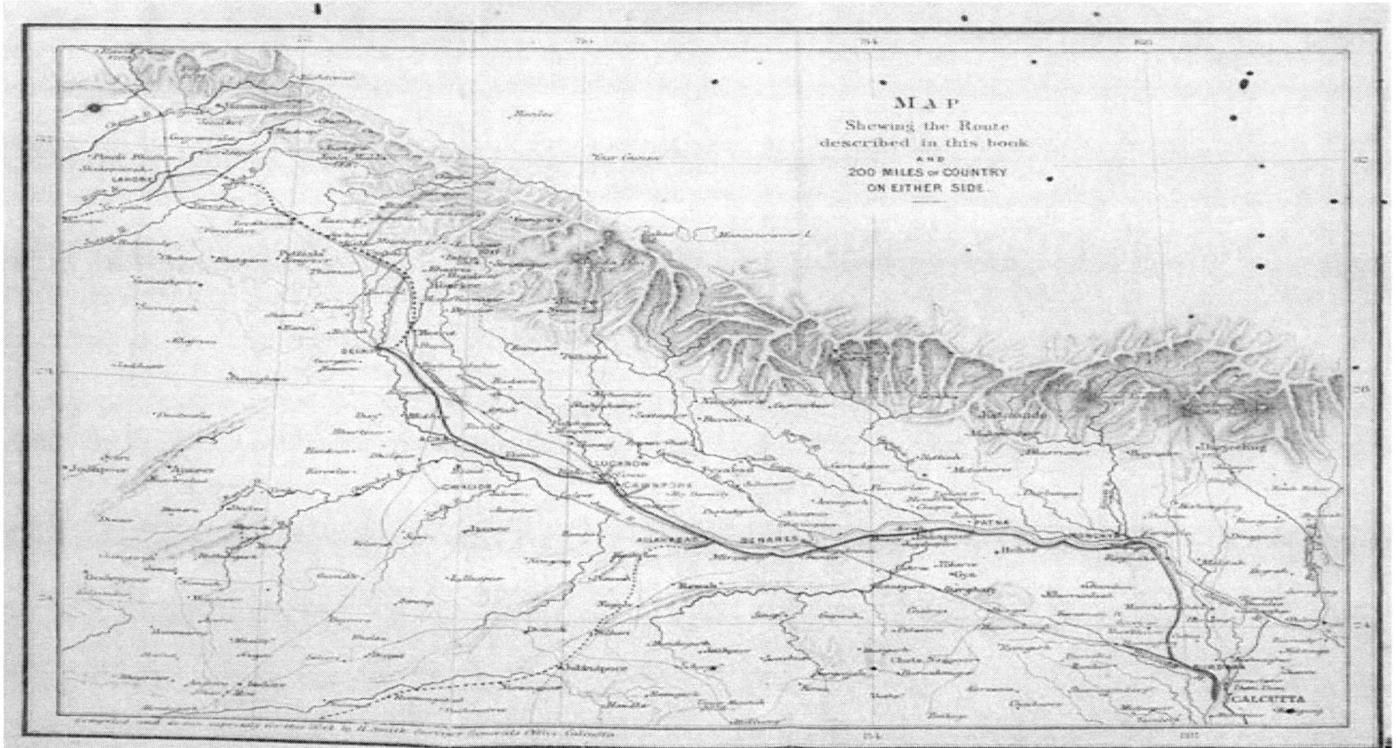
MAP
Shewing the Route
described in this book
AND
200 MILES OF COUNTRY
ON EITHER SIDE.
LAHORE
DELHI
LUCKNOW
CAWNPORE
ALLAHABAD
BENARES
PATNA
CALCUTTA

CALCUTTA TO THE SNOWY RANGE.

CHAPTER I.

INTRODUCTORY.

Want of a Calcutta Railway-terminus. — Winter in the Plains and the Provinces.—Through Railway to Delhi. —Sleeping-carriages. — Requisites for the Journey.— Indian Refreshment-rooms. — Wherewithal for the Journey. — Indian Railway-stations. — Native Passengers. — Railway-accidents. — An Indian Railway-carriage. — Delights of Summer-travel. — Engine-drivers.

THE world is now so familiarized with travel, and people so *au fait* regarding all the particulars of a journey from London to anywhere, that I should be nervous of my chance of obtaining a hearing, except at the hands perhaps of Indian residents, were my starting point the great Metropolis itself. As it happens I have in one respect distanced competition by beginning where many would claim to leave off — at a distance of several thousand miles from home.

For this reason it is believed that few will be found so familiar with the scenes and places described, as to render a perusal of this Work otherwise than instructive and it is hoped interesting as well.

Although it is probable that few in England — even though accustomed to travel — will follow my steps, it is certain that many in India, from business, necessity, or pleasure, are likely to do so; and while, from the great strangeness of the places described rather than from the power of description, I may hope to create an interest with the former, I must trust to the utility of the Work, as well, to find more permanent favour with the latter.

Even if I pretended to describe the journey to Calcutta by the Overland Route—long and serious as it is—the affair is now so well understood that such detail would be superfluous. I make no apology therefore for starting, in accordance with my title, direct "from Calcutta to the Snowy Range."

It was in the month of February, 1865, that, in fulfilment of a long-felt desire to see somewhat more of India than many years' residence there had hitherto permitted, I found myself, with an agreeable companion, waiting for the Train at the Calcutta terminus * of the E. I. Railway, *en route* for the Upper Provinces on a holiday tour. I had received a friendly warning that I should soon find the heat a great hindrance to pleasure; but the experience of the trip showed me that a more agreeable time for such a journey, as far as the Plains are concerned, could hardly have been chosen; for, since the "winter" lasts longer Up-country than in Calcutta, by starting thus late I secured as it were fully an additional month of cold weather. On my return to Calcutta at the end of March, I found the hot weather fully set in, and punkahs in full swing, whereas but a few days previously, at Umballa and Delhi, I had been glad to resort at night to blankets.

It must not, however, be supposed, from this, that there is a very much longer cold season in the Upper Provinces than in Bengal. I believe the duration of the monsoons is much the same; but there is some variation in the respective provinces, in the times of advent

* This is, perhaps, a misnomer; for, strange to say, the terminus still remains in the suburb of Howrah, separated from Calcutta by the formidable Hooghly River, to the inconvenience—not to say danger—of every city resident.

departure. The cold is, however, keener Up-country; and although the heat is of a drier nature than in Bengal, and felt more severely in the day there than in the Lower Provinces, the temperature falls considerably before and after sundown. Thus, from the practice prevailing of keeping in-doors during the day, the heat is not so much felt as in Bengal—*khus-khus tatties*,* during the prevalence of the hot winds, greatly lessening the inconvenience of this visitation.

It is not very long ago that the traveller undertaking the expedition I am now about to describe, would, after a few hours' rail journey to Raneegunge (for a long time the furthermost railway point) have composedly taken his seat in the ever-to-be-remembered *dâk gharry*, not from thence to be displaced until he reached his journey's end. *Mais nous avons changé tout cela.* Now, we do not require to change carriages till arrival in the North-western Provinces; and even this hindrance has, since these papers were written, been removed, and the traveller is enabled to run through direct from

* Blinds made of a sweet-smelling, dried grass, so called. They are kept constantly wet, and the hot air from without, tempered by entering through them, diffuses a delightful, though dangerous, coolness over the apartment.

Calcutta to Delhi. As railway travelling forms so essential an element of the Indian journey nowadays, it is as well that I should refer to it beforehand.

Although, in India, this method of locomotion is by no means so luxurious as at home and on the Continent, it possesses two advantages,—the one, that, in the 1st class you are by no means incommoded with fellow-passengers; the other, that in long distances you have the luxury of a sleeping-carriage; that is, a carriage fitted with conveniences, and in which the cushions at the back can be strapped up to the roof so as to form a bed. When thus arranged, the carriage affords sleeping accommodation for four persons. The luxury of this can be readily imagined.

Notwithstanding that in travelling much baggage is proverbially a nuisance, you must in India by no means omit to carry with you a *resai* (a stuffed cotton quilt), a pillow, and a railway-rug. The night's rest passed in the railway-carriage is considerably improved by the addition to the carriage-cushion of your *resai* and pillow, while in the rug you have a very necessary protection in the winter months from the cold night-air, the temperature after sundown being totally out of comparison with what one might suppose it would be, judging from that of the day. It will also be seen hereafter why these articles are, for other reasons, indispensable. An umbrella and a *solah topee* (or Indian sun-helmet) are also necessary adjuncts. Careless as one may be of the matter in England, your portmanteaus, too, must be small and few enough to go under the seat of the carriage, unless you would incur the delay and trouble probably of an open-air inspection of the luggage-van.

Most unfairly, I think, the cost of 1st class travelling in India is precisely double that of the 2nd, whilst the charge in the 3rd class is disproportionately small—on a par, nevertheless, with the accommodation afforded. The rate of the former is thus prohibitory to many, but the distances to be traversed are so long, and the fatigue in a tropical climate so considerable, that one cannot afford to dispense with the extra comfort secured by the better-provided carriages of the 1st class; not to mention the fact that in the 2nd class you are quite liable to have as a travelling companion some half-clothed native, redolent of unsavoury odours, — respectable though he may be.

I have travelled much on railways in England

and France, but have never experienced anything approaching the dust and glare of an Indian line. I was fortunately careful to provide myself with "eye-protectors"—either these or a veil being highly necessary. There is another little precaution which well repays the trouble of carriage,—a small bag containing towel, soap, and sponge, with brush and comb. The luxury of an occasional ablution, although taken *al fresco* at the carriage-door, is not to be over-estimated.

At almost every Station water can be got —to wash with, not to drink; although the *bheestie* may generally be seen running up and down the station platform with a greasy *mussuck* (water-skin) on his back, employed in filling the glasses of such thirsty passengers as are foolish enough to partake of this "cholera mixture," and who may have thoughtlessly neglected to provide themselves at starting with that most necessary appendage —a wicker-work water-bottle of *aqua vitæ* and *aqua pura* mildly combined, or with the latter only, as taste dictates.

For anything like a long distance, the experienced traveller, in lieu of depending on the railway refreshment-rooms, provides himself with a small box containing such eatables, drinkables, and necessary accompaniments as are likely to be needed on the road. One is thus able to take such refreshment as is required, *when* one requires it, and in comparative ease and comfort. The pretence of a meal at the refreshment-room, in the limited and uncertain time allowed you for it, only results in spoiling your digestion, souring your temper, and diminishing unnecessarily the contents of your purse. And if the traveller happens to arrive at night, the prospect becomes still more dismal and uncomfortable. Ye newly-arrived Indians who remember the brilliantly-lighted refreshment - saloon of Wolverhampton, or of any large station at home, with its smiling attendant handmaids, its scalding-hot coffee, and its seductively-arranged patties; with its counter covered with delicacies — the genial sight of all which makes you regret the return to your now cheerless-looking carriage—forget all this when you travel on Indian lines, and picture to yourself instead, what you will assuredly witness:—a large, comfortless-looking room, found with difficulty; an apology for a *carpet* on the floor, in shape of a dirty piece of stripe-coloured canvas; a broken-down plated candlestick (or perhaps two) on the table, the glass shade covering which is as innocent of having undergone the cleansing process as is the linen of the half-awake attendant Khitmutgar, who rouses himself reluctantly from a snooze on the floor, just as you, in despair, have decided to return supperless to your carriage. And then, if tempted by the greasy curry and half-cold chops, the leathery steak or hashed unmentionable in the dish with the cracked cover, the tough old bantam or unsavoury-looking stew in ditto of another pattern, you *do* venture to appease your hunger, be sure that before you have had time thoroughly to discover all the drawbacks of such a repast, the bell for starting will ring, and you will hurry off, hardly waiting for your change, fearful lest you be left behind at the Station, where desolation reigns supreme, discomfort everywhere, and at which, most probably, passenger-trains upwards stop but once a day.*

The traveller in England can choose pretty well to his fancy as regards his resting-place on a long journey; but, in the cold season in India, if you are wise, make up your mind, before starting, where you will halt on the

* A favourable exception to the rule is the refreshment-room at Allahabad; and, indeed, these remarks apply more particularly to the Stations *above* this place. Since this was written, I learn that in these some improvement has been effected. It is to be hoped so.

journey, and at what hotels you wish to put up, securing quarters at such in advance. You are otherwise almost certain to be disappointed in obtaining accommodation.

Also, as to the wherewithal for the journey. In England it is only necessary to have enough of it; but in the East, though gold is now a legal tender, and currency notes in circulation all over India, it is not every Up-country native who will receive your sovereign as 10 rs., or every "Circle" that will take the notes of another without discount. You take, therefore, say a third of your cash in gold, as much silver as convenient, and notes (in due proportion) of the "Circles" through which you pass.* A good supply of *small* coin is also found very desirable, and saves you from throwing away annas where pice would suffice, or rupees where annas would answer equally.

Although the distances between the principal Stations are very great, there are innumerable petty halting places, necessitating a constant reference to your time-table in order to ascertain your whereabouts, and disturbing many a

* Indian currency notes are divided amongst so many "Circles," to prevent an over-accumulation of bullion at one place, and to give the natives confidence in the ability of the head office of a "Circle" at any time to cash notes from the specie kept in reserve for this purpose.

comfortable "forty winks." Even on English lines, it is almost a matter of impossibility to understand the name of the Station as shouted forth by the attendant porter; but judge what is likely to be the state of the case in India, where the lanky yellow-capped and slippershod "Peon" (answering to the designation of a train-porter at home), looking the very picture of helplessness, yells out in barbaric manner some such euphonious name as *Kanchrapara*, or *Srishnanuggur;* * meanwhile, to render matters more intelligible, clanging his bell, announcing the approach of the train, while it is actually drawing alongside the platform.

The majority of the Stations on the East-India Railway are shamefully deficient in accommodation for passengers. Indeed, the accommodation provided is, as a rule, a desolate-looking room, furnished with an uncovered and dirty table in the centre, and a row of forms round the wall; all generally so thick with dust, that you could write in it a history of your sufferings.

* In the Appendix (No. 1) is given a list of all the Stations up to Delhi, showing the distance between each, the time occupied in transit, and the fares; and I will forgive the reader if he can pronounce correctly one half the names.

Notwithstanding the severity of the weather, too, in India, to Europeans, many of the smaller Stations have no covering. The practice, also, of permitting a horde of filthy coolies to scramble for your luggage, in place of the wholesome English plan of the Railway Company employing ticket-porters, is equally reprehensible.

For economy's sake the greater part of the Station-masters are natives, as are also the whole of the railway police. But a very false economy it proves, as is attested by the innumerable accidents which take place, and the delays and frequent robberies of goods and parcels which occur.

The Stations themselves along the line are at night miserably lighted; and unless you are very careful, you will come into collision, on alighting to stretch your limbs, with one of many stray packages and huge bundles of native wraps and cloths, invariably left by the Up-country travelling aborigines exactly where they should not be; while their unfortunate owners rush about in wild excitement and confusion, followed helplessly by their women and children, in search of the 3rd or 4th class ticket-office, before which a seething, unsavoury crowd of struggling passengers are fighting for place, the baboo or clerk behind the partition dispensing tickets by the light of a dirty *chiragh*,* with irritating slowness, utterly regardless of the Babel going on around him.

Most of us remember the sight and have shared in the struggle of a London crowd before a railway ticket-office. There, however, the demonstrations are comparatively silent, though not always painless; but a native crowd goes on the principle of making up for lack of muscular demonstration by the energy of their vocal uproar. From all parts of the oily human throng—now compressed, now expanding, with the very elasticity of India-rubber—are heard deafening shouts, relieved occasionally by a moving appeal to the "babö-ö," dimly visible on the other side of the pigeon-hole: one bewailing that he has no ticket, and will be too late for the train; another holding up strugglingly aloft a pass for Benares he has by mistake received instead of one for Allahabad; a third tendering, over the heads of others, beseechingly but unavailingly, his pice; whilst his neighbour, with empty outstretched palm, screamingly demands his change. All this perhaps in a mixture of

* A cotton wick in an earthen saucer filled with oil.

dialects, and certainly a Babel of tongues, may be seen at almost every Station where there is anything like a rush (as there nearly always is) of native passengers.

At sound of the warning words "*Guntah maro!*—Ring the bell!"—the crowd with one accord instantly dissolves, and in scampering broken groups is seen wildly rushing to and fro on the platform; pelting helter-skelter as if for very life into the pens provided for them, where, stowed away much after the fashion of tightly-packed herrings, they are at leisure to enjoy the comforts of European locomotion, and whiff their hubble-bubble in stolid indifference.

The rate of travelling on Indian lines seldom exceeds twenty miles an hour; mainly, I suppose, on account of the Stations being very close together, and trains stopping at all of them for the convenience of the many native passengers, the number of whom availing themselves of this mode of travelling constitutes the chief source of income of the Company. At one time the natives, as a class, hesitated to use the rail, the bugbear caste suggesting numberless objections; but time and necessity have altered this, and now the native passenger-traffic on all parts of the line attests the "enlightenment," so far, of the most backward, apathetic, and obstructive people in the world. This readiness to avail themselves of an advantage they have done naught towards creating, is, amongst natives, in the case of railway-travelling, accompanied by no little self-denial in the matter of personal comfort; and I should hardly think it would be money ill spent were something like a sufficiency of room provided by the not too liberal East-India Railway Company for its 3rd and 4th class passengers.

For the greater part of its length, the railway has but a single line; and this, owing to the excessive traffic, and the want of due attention to orders on the part of Native Station-masters, is a most fruitful source of accidents.* No less than three such occurred on my trip,—one attended with loss of life; whilst in another, I found myself in the night suddenly precipitated from the sleeping-compartment to the floor: carriage-lamp, bottles, bags, and boxes tumbling wildly over and about us. Creeping half-stunned out of the carriage window, I inquired, "What

* The official returns of accidents on the East-India Railway show that, during the year 1863, 26 persons were killed and 14 injured, in a total of 24 accidents, 21 of which are stated as "*attributable to the negligence of servants.*" The number of miles of line over which this "little Bill" is divisible was only 924 ! !

was the matter?" "Oh," said the guard, "it's only a goods train run into us—no harm done." The third instance was that of an engine and file of carriages running beyond the rails into the Jumna river. The cost in money, attending two of these incidents, was stated at some two lacs of rupees (£20,000). This, if not the care for life, would, one might fairly presume, have called serious public attention to the matter; but beyond a paragraph in the papers recording the accidents, nothing further, I believe, publicly transpired. Government has recently sanctioned the doubling of the line for a much greater length, and this will doubtless remedy the evil so far.

In connection with a railway journey to so distant a spot as Delhi, the query may not unnaturally arise in the mind of the English reader as to what an Indian railway-carriage is like, and whether any special provision is made against the effects of climate in a place where exposure to the sun is so dangerous. And it will, perhaps, not be out of place if, in this introductory chapter, I touch upon that point. The train, as it stands drawn up by the platform, with its bright-polished engine shining brilliantly in the sun, and snorting impatiently in puffs of curly steam, is at a first glance uncommonly like a railway-train in England or anywhere else. But a new-comer would soon discover a difference. The carriages are, to begin with, very much stronger, larger, and loftier, and are protected from the sun by a double roof—the upper one a few inches removed from the lower, and projecting slightly on either side. Then, to every window there are, in addition to the glasses, Venetian blinds, and to the first-class carriages frequently sun-shades besides; ventilation is also specially and very necessarily provided for: indeed, as far as is possible, the carriages are built for the climate. But what avail double roof, Venetian blinds, or sun-shade, against the terrible sun of an Indian summer! Then the carriages become, as it were, red-hot; and entering one is like going into a heated furnace. You soon assume a listless, half wrung-out appearance, and keep yourself amused by mopping up the perspiration, as it freely pours from you. The very seat is hot to the touch; and you refrain from leaning back, lest your coat stick to the varnished panel. If, as is devoutly to be wished, no ladies are present, you relapse into the free-and-easy, take off the boots from your swollen feet, denude yourself of coat and waistcoat, unfasten your soaked collar, and hang it up to dry, put your feet at a comfortable angle on the opposite cushion, elevated, if possible, to a level with your nose, light your cheroot, and, stimulated by a "peg" (which is *brandy-shrab and belatee-panee*, which is soda and brandy), dreamily subside into a patient endurance of the miseries of a long Indian summer railway journey.

I cannot assign a reason for smoking making one cooler; but I affirm that it does so, and that is, I suppose, why people in hot climates smoke so much. And, again, the apparently idle habit of putting your feet on a level with your head,—there is a good deal in that, too. But I *can* explain why this affords relief, and is a habit so readily and universally indulged in in tropical countries:—the blood, over-heated, flows rapidly to the extremities; thus, by the orthodox Indian fashion of placing your feet on the table or thereabouts, the legs and feet are necessarily relieved by the blood being sent back.

But to resume, if railway-travelling in hot weather is so irksome to the traveller, what must it be to the engine-driver? For, of course, he is a European like yourself. You feel very sorry for him; but you would not care to trust yourself with a native driver, either — not exactly. True, however, to the law that the supply is always equal to the demand, dangerous and trying as must be the duty, plenty are found willing, for the additional emolument and privileges offered, to undertake it.* And I am told that fewer casualties from exposure occur than might reasonably be supposed. The engine is provided with a thick roof over that part where the men stand, and the current of air caused by rushing along so rapidly mitigates the heat. Native stokers are also provided. Nevertheless, perfect sobriety — almost abstinence — is a *sine qua non* for fitness for the duty, which, in any case, must be of a most taxing kind to a European; and often as I have pitied the driver of an English train, on a biting winter night, I believe the exposure is as nothing compared to the effects of the scorching blaze of an Eastern sun.

We will now suppose ourselves seated in the train, — not by any means, be it understood, suffering at this time of the year from the evils just described. And so, having once more sworn at our cooly, still clamouring for double

* The mechanic *employés* of the East-Indian Railway Company are well cared for in respect to dwellings, large blocks of buildings having been specially erected for them; they also enjoy many privileges not dreamt of in work-a-day England.

his hire as he chases the train along the platform, the thoroughly English-looking guard gives the final signal; and the lanky, yellow-capped native porter having frantically waved once more to the nervous pointsman ahead, off we start, — the usual crowd of native men, women, and boys, vacantly gazing at us as we shoot past.

CHAPTER II.

CALCUTTA TO MONGHYR.

The Railway-track in Bengal. — An Indian Village. — Effects of the Cyclone.—Places *en route*.—The Maharajah of Burdwan.— Plassey. — Monghyr: its Salubrity; Hot Wells.—Benares, the Holy City.

IN Bengal, the railway-track lies for the most part through a well-cultivated but intensely flat and marshy plain—rice-fields stretching for miles around, with here and there a patch of pawn cultivation (betel-nut), the landscape relieved only by a few thickly-covered stumpy trees or clump of brushwood.

Occasionally we come upon a native village. They are all alike. What a tumble-down look it has! Its thatched roofs sloping up and down in all sorts of imaginable curves, looking as if they had not quite made up their minds on which side to topple over. The doorway of each hut is only just high enough, you see, to get in at, although there is a little more elevation inside. No ugly chimney-stacks here. The smoke follows nature's law, and gets out the quickest way it can through the roof. Smoke, the natives say, kills mosquitoes. It is perhaps as well that it does; for the deep moat which surrounds the huts of the village, with its few inches' depth of rather sluggish water — unpleasantly black-looking — is calculated to breed mosquitoes and the like somewhat rapidly. I never could make out why the little plank of wood, or trunk of a tree, which spans this moat and serves as a bridge to the dwelling, should so invariably be chosen by the members of the family as the spot, above all others, whereon to perform the operation of teeth-cleaning. It cannot be that the odour from the ditch is *appetizing*, even if it be (as, of course, it is) malarious. The fact of the floors, too, being composed of mud can hardly conduce to the health of the habitants; especially as there is no drainage, excepting the moat aforesaid. True, a great many are stricken with fever, and numbers die; but as there is sure to be a fire or two in the hot season, that probably is considered to be a sufficient purification.* "Our villager" is rather obstinate in sanitary matters—or rather the neglect of them. He does not believe in drainage, besides objecting to the cost. I doubt if he would even let you make the place wholesome, if you paid for it yourself. In that irregular line of bamboo-and-mat erections dwell quite a colony of people. You would not at all appreciate their number in the daytime. All is still and somnolent — even the trees. The males are probably out in the fields, while their better halves are asleep, and the *bābā-loq* (children) at school. But look at the village in the early morning or in the decline of the day: you will wonder how it is possible for so many to be accommodated in so few and such small habitations. However dull and listless the village may have seemed in the noontide

* In the outskirts of Calcutta, village conflagrations are fearfully numerous, and are supposed, more often than not, to be the work of incendiary *guārāmees*—men whose trade is building in bamboo and thatch, and who thus secure for themselves a good stroke of business. A municipal enactment now compels all huts, in the limits of the town of Calcutta, to be tiled and covered with mud. Previously, fires were almost as frequent in the city as the suburbs.

heat, all now is bustle and clamour: children noisily playing, chattering, and making little mud-pies — a favourite amusement even in India; the village "lasses" gathering cow-dung to manufacture into fuel; paterfamilias washing himself and his linen in the weed-covered piece of water fronting the village, —a pond which serves alike all purposes of ablution and drinking; his better half filling therefrom the water-jars or cooking the family meal; vendors of grain, curry-stuff, and wood, bargaining—you would think, to listen, quarrelling; a knot of eager gossips discussing village concerns in a highly declamatory manner; pariah dogs barking, cows lowing, kids bleating, while the parent goat, chased by her owner, is having a run for it before consenting to give her usual supply of *dood* (milk); here the village barber carefully removing yesterday's growth of hair from the poll of that slightly-clad gentleman sitting so wondrously on his haunches, while a Brahmin opposite, chiefly remarkable for his filthiness, daubs a would-be dandy with a finishing touch of ochre on his nose, face, and ears. If it be evening, you will probably hear the tom-tom discoursing sweet music, or the clanging of native cymbals, and other "instruments of music" (resembling, in effect, the beating of a household of pots and pans),* to celebrate some wedding or festival.

As the train — the "fire-carriage," as we have it in Hindoostanee—whirls past, from out the village come little groups of swarthy naked imps to gaze at it; while the head of the family we left standing up to his waist in the green dank pond, for a moment ceases the cleansing process of plastering himself with mud, to gaze stolidly at what to him is now hardly a novelty, though still much of a mystery, — which, however, he has not the remotest desire to solve.

Almost as far as Burdwan the country showed, to within a few months back, fearful evidence of the devastating cyclone which recently swept so violently over Calcutta and the neighbourhood. The force of the storm was more immediately expended in and near Calcutta, sinking and stranding 150 noble vessels, and all the small craft of the river; levelling, beyond hope of restoration, the glorious century-old giants in the Botanical Gardens and Barrackpore Park, — the like

* The natives say that the English excel them in all things but one—*music!* They like a brass band, however,—that is,—the drum.

of which we can hardly hope to see again, and reducing the appearance of Calcutta to that of a city after a bombardment. But even for miles in the outskirts, hundreds of grand and lofty trees were entirely uprooted; while such as escaped total destruction, more by their pliability than their strength, are seen bowed and twisted in all directions and shapes, and it is doubtful if they will ever recover their original appearance. Anyhow, many years must elapse before the injury done to the country in this respect can be repaired.

A pleasant run through the green plain before described, past the old-fashioned missionary station of Serampore, Dutch all over—the scene of the labours of Carey, Marshman, and Ward; next by the French settlement of Chandernagore, with its Governor on a salary of £500 a year, and its regiment of 52 sepoys — the Alsatia of refuge for Calcutta folks afflicted with the troubles of impecuniosity, — a cleanly pleasant little place withal — brings you in a couple of hours to Burdwan, the residence, and principality it may be said, of the Maharajah of that name. This native prince possesses here a vast domain, 73 miles in length by 40 in breadth, of great wealth, and is an enlightened and liberal gentleman. His palace and grounds are very beautiful, and are thrown freely open to visitors. Most Europeans residing in or near Calcutta make a special excursion to Burdwan, for the purpose of inspecting the place, which is well worthy a visit, and comprises a capital menagerie.

Those whom the Maharajah delights to honour are invited to take up their abode for as long as they please, in a building specially devoted to the purpose, and are, whilst thus the guests of his highness, most hospitably entertained. The Maharajah is a Hindoo, and as such unable to eat with Christians; but he, nevertheless, provides frequent and liberal entertainments and balls, to which the civilians and principal European residents of the Station are freely invited.

Burdwan has had its part in the eventful times of one and two centuries ago. It was at one time the residence of Shah Jehan, sustained a siege from the Moguls in 1621, and was, in 1743, the encamping-ground of a Mahratta army of 120,000 men. But more especially may be mentioned the fact, that it was from Burdwan, in 1695, that the English factors received the lease of the ground on which Calcutta now stands—this small company of "merchants trading to the East Indies," which has since held sovereignty over the Empire of India, and from whom ultimately the Rajah of Benares himself was only too content to hold in vassalage his vast possessions.*

Burdwan is a highly cultivated and flourishing district, but there is little else of interest in or about it than what I have mentioned. We then enter the train again and pass on, through the same dead level tract of paddy-land and brushwood, the glimpse of an occasional graceful palm reminding us that we are not in the marshes of Essex.

A short distance behind Burdwan is a branch line leading to Raneegunge, the coal-field of Bengal. Next we cross the rivers More and Adjai, in Bheerboom; and pass, at Cynthia, near Clive's battle-field of Plassey, where, in 1757, the fortunes of the day went so largely towards establishing the footing of the British in Bengal.

By this time, dusty as a miller, thirsty as Mynheer, and tired as you can well desire,

* The British Government now receive a rental of some £400,000 for the lands over which the present Maharajah claims zemindaree rights.

having travelled some 200 miles almost straight as the crow flies — grinding up, as the iron horse ploughs along the shiny track, a very atmosphere of sharp penetrating dust, you come at length in sight of a low dark-looking range of hills. These pertain to the Rajmehal range, inhabited by the two hill tribes, the Patarins and the Santhals—the latter easily distinguished by their woolly hair, thick lips, flat noses, and muscular strength, and often armed with bow and arrows, or a hatchet. Shortly after passing Teen Pehar and Sahibgunge (the nearest railway point to Darjeeling), where the Ganges proper is first seen, you reach the old Station of Bhaugulpoor, — a cleanly and highly salubrious spot—now the Mofussil residence of the Lieutenant-Governor of Bengal. Eighty miles farther on is the Station of Jumalpore, rather an important junction: and from this point a branch line leads to Monghyr—a place to which I found it well worth while to pay a visit. Monghyr is a pretty green spot, very English in appearance, and much resorted to by Calcutta residents on account of its salubrity. The residences are principally within the Fort, now scarcely visible, whose ramparts, covered with greenest grass, look cheerful and refreshing to the dust-stained and already weary traveller.

There is, however, but one hotel (or, more properly speaking, boarding-house) in the place. This is mostly full; and at the time of my visit it was crammed. Having come so long and wearisome a journey, and it being then dusk, I offered to make up my bed on the dining-table, rather than be obliged to continue my journey that night. Unfortunately, an equally necessitous traveller had been before me, and I was fain to trudge back to the Jumalpore Station, and undergo the no slight penance of waiting for six hours, in the middle of the night, in the desolate apartments there, with a perfect colony of musquitoes for company!

Thornton thus describes Monghyr: "The town comprises sixteen markets, scattered over a space a mile and a half long from north to south, and a mile wide. The houses are generally small: they have sloping roofs of red tiles, and gables ornamented with earthenware figures. It is a thriving place, having a great number of manufactories and shops for the fabrication and sale of hardware and fire-arms, but of execrable quality. The view of the town from the river is agreeable; it appears ornamented with numerous gay Hindoo temples; and the effect of the whole is highly picturesque. The fort, built on a prominent rock, is partly washed by the Ganges, and where this is not the case, its rampart is defended on the outside by a wide deep ditch. The length of the fort from north to south is about 4,000 feet, the breadth 3,500; it contains three large tanks, and many residences and offices of the civil establishment; it is also a Military Station. It is a favourite place of residence for invalided military men and their families, being considered highly salubrious, and also very agreeable, from the beauty of the surrounding scenery. The rock jutting into the river is considered sacred by the Hindoos; and at certain seasons vast numbers of pilgrims enter the river for the purpose of ritual ablution. Formerly there was, directly above the bathing-place, a handsome Brahminical temple, which was converted into a mosque by Shooja, son of Shajehan. Within the fort is another mosque, beautifully built of black marble. The ruins of a splendid palace, built by Sultan Shooja, may still be traced; and contiguous is a vast well, always abundantly replenished, and believed to have a subterraneous communication with the Ganges.

"It probably was at an early period a place

of strength, but the construction of the present fort is generally attributed to Husain, styled by Buchanan the greatest of the kings of Bengal. It was repaired and enlarged, about 1660, by Shooja, son of Shajehan, at the commencement of his unsuccessful struggle for empire and life against his brother Aurungzebe. It was subsequently repaired by Cossim Ali, when preparing for hostilities against the East-India Company. His precautions, however, availed not, as, after a feeble resistance of a few days' continuance, it was captured by the British. It was then considered a place of consequence as a stronghold in regard to its proximity to the north-west frontier; but the removal of that boundary to so great a distance has rendered it of no importance in such a point of view."

Monghyr still answers in many respects to the foregoing description, save that it is no longer a Military Station (a jail guard only being quartered there), and that its fort is recognized only by the remains of high earthworks — now sloping mounds — covered by greenest grass. But looking at this pretty, countrified, unpretending little place, one finds it difficult in the present time to realize sufficiently the state of things which the extract given above indicates.

A few miles' pleasant drive from Monghyr, at a spot called Seetacoond, are some hot springs, well worth a visit. They are held in great sanctity by the natives of the place, groups of whom may be seen laving themselves with apparent enjoyment in the coolest of the steamy sulphurous basins. The wells are built in with masonry, and are approached each by a broad flight of steps, above which crumble the remains of an old temple. The water is of a pale bluish tinge; and looking down through its transparent depth, the rocky boulders at the bottom glisten, as if silvered, with the escaping gases. In some of the springs, the water is so hot as to render painful the immersion of the hand; and as the myriad gaseous bubbles rise sparkling to the surface, emitting each its tiny column of vapour, the effect is at once peculiar and striking.

But it is a long way to Delhi, so let us get into the train again to return to Jumalpore—now the principal locomotive depôt of the East-India Railway Company, and with its large workshops and dwellings resembling another Crewe. Rushing along, scaring the lazy cows, and bringing out more semi-nude villagers to gaze at us, we pass the city of Patna and the military post of Dinapore, which, closely adjoining one another, form together on the banks of the Ganges some miles of continuous buildings. Next is reached the river Soane (a mighty stream in the freshes), spanned by the wondrous latticed iron-girder bridge of nearly a mile long: passing Arrah, in zillah Shahabad, the scene of the gallant defence of a handful against the five mutinous regiments from Dinapore; also crossing the river Kurramnassa, the geographical boundary between Bengal and the North-western Provinces; and leaving behind Buxar, with its long line of Government stables for horse-breeding and rearing, we arrive at the next principal halting-place — Mogul Serai, another junction 236 miles distant from the last. Here is a branch line to Benares, the renowned and Holy City of the Hindoos, which, as a recent writer in the *Calcutta Review* remarks, "By reason of some subtle and mysterious charm, has linked itself with the religious sympathies of the Hindus through every century of its existence. For the sanctity of its inhabitants, of its temples and tanks, of its wells and streams, of the very soil that is trodden, of the very air that is breathed, and of everything in it and around it, Benares has been famed for thousands of years. The poor deluded sensualist, whose life has been passed in abominable practices; or the covetous *mahajan*, who has made himself rich by a long course of hard-fisted extortion; or the fanatical devotee, fool and murderer, more simple than a babe, yet guilty of the foulest crimes, still comes as of old from the remotest corners of India, as the sands of time are slowly ebbing away; and fearful lest the golden thread should be snapped before his long journey is ended, he makes desperate efforts to hold on his course, until, arriving at the sacred city and touching its hallowed soil, his anxious spirit becomes suddenly calm, comforted with the relief that comes over him, and he is at once cheered and comforted with the treacherous lie, that his sins are forgiven, and his soul is saved."

Dirty as it is, and possessing little, if any, of strictly European interest, it is nevertheless a truly remarkable place,—the focus of Brahminical superstition; the most thoroughly *native* city, perhaps, in all India; and the one of all others comprising the largest population in the smallest compass,—being estimated to contain no less than 300,000 inhabitants.

CHAPTER III.

BENARES.

Benares: The Bridge of Boats.—Letters of Introduction. — Etymology of the word Benares.— Idolatry of the People; their dirty Cleanliness.—The Holy Ganges.— The Golden Pagoda.—The Well of Knowledge.—Mankarnika.—Ancient Hindu Observatory.—The Ghats of Benares. — The Mosque of Aurungzebe. — Buddhist Monument. — The Monkey Temple. — The Benares Opium-Agency.

STARTING from the large and somewhat pretentious Station at Mogul Serai, the train lands you on this side of Benares in about twenty minutes. The river is crossed here by that most shaky and antiquated contrivance—a bridge of boats. To cross this bridge, you have to pay the moderate toll of *two rupees* (four shillings)! and unless you are careful to make a *bunderbust* (arrangement) before starting, to this will have to be added a sum of *four* rupees to take you into the Civil lines, some four miles distant. The proper fare is, however, two rupees, notwithstanding that a printed handbill, thrust into your hand at the Station, defines the fare to be double. Being unable, by dint either of threats or persuasions, to induce the obdurate Jehu to agree for less, I paid this amount, under a strong mental protest, of course, to find out afterwards the trick that had been played.

In Calcutta we have at length arrived—but only very recently—at the high state of civilization indicated by a "Hackney Carriage Act;" and it is proved to be equally beneficial to the employed and to the public. Up-country, however, you lose what few civilizing specialities Calcutta does possess, and are absolutely at the mercy of the native, whether he be a *garrywan* (cabman) or anything else.

A friend is nowhere more likely to be one in "need" than at Benares, and letters of introduction are not in this instance, at any rate (as they often are), an unnecessary formality. You soon learn to forego all modesty in accepting an hospitable offer to put you up; for there is but one hotel (save the mark!) in the place, and a small dâk bungalow, always full.

Highly interesting as Benares is in an historical point of view, and situated as it is so close to the Presidency, it has, nevertheless, till recently, been almost a *terra incognita* to Europeans; and few, save those passing through it on business, have taken the trouble to explore the city,—these even probably seeking little acquaintance with its history. The facilities now afforded by the rail, however, cannot fail to attract a large number of visitors to the place; and it may soon be considered as necessary to "do" Benares as it now is Agra and Delhi.

General Cunningham, in his Archæological Survey Report, published by the Asiatic Society of Bengal, thus accurately describes the situation of Benares, and furnishes the etymology of the name by which it is universally known. He says:—"The city of Benares is situated on the left bank of the Ganges. The points of the junction of both streams with the Ganges are considered particularly holy, and, accordingly, temples have been erected both at *Barna Saugaur*, below the city, and at *Así Saugaur*, above the city. From the joint names of these two streams, which bound the city to the north and south, the Brahmins derive 'Varanasi,' which is said to be the Sanscrit form of the name of Benares. But the more usual derivative amongst the common people is from Rajah *Banar*, who is said to have rebuilt the city about 800 years ago."

Contrary to what is found elsewhere in India,

the lapse of time and the influx of European civilization seem in no sense to have altered the condition of things existing at the time Benares was ceded to us,—in 1755. Superstition and bigotry of the intensest kind still reign supreme; and, judging from the number of temples everywhere abounding, the innumerable attendant priests and ever-present devotees, one might presume that the business of the inhabitants was little else than one continued *poojah* to idolatry. Indeed, a recent writer in the *Calcutta Review*—one well versed in his subject,—says: "The love for idolatry is so deep-seated and intense in the breast of the Hindu, that it is a common thing for both men and women to amuse themselves, with a pious intent, with manufacturing little gods from mud or clay, and after paying divine honours to them (and that too with the same profound reverence which they display in their devotions before the well-known deities of the temples), to throw them away."

This city presents a very imposing appearance from the Raj Ghat Railway Station, where the whole may be taken in at a view. It is only on approaching the city over the bridge of boats that a correct estimate may be formed of its distinctive features, its ghauts, temples,

BENARES.

and massive edifices, some even six or seven stories high; whilst one object above all stands out amongst the pile upon pile of buildings—the Great Mosque of Aurungzebe, with its stately minarets, marking, as it were, for all time, the triumph of the religion of the Crescent over the despised and debasing superstitions of an abject and prostrate people.

The illustration facing this page is from the pencil of a native artist, and although it fails to give as imposing and comprehensive a view of the river-face of the town as some I have seen, I have selected it in preference to a more artistically rendered production, because it is the work of a native. The listless laziness of the groups in the foreground is admirably portrayed, as also the curious sitting posture so peculiar to the native of India. A little to the right of the drawing, in very bad perspective, rises the lofty ascent of the Madhoray Ghat, the hundred steps of which are worn into holes and curves by the feet of the many thousands who, for centuries past, have ascended and descended to and from the sacred stream which turbidly flows at foot.

To see the city, the stranger has but one of three methods before him, if he has little time on his hands; but if he has that to spare, he may employ all three, and thus "do" the city quite leisurely. The first of these is by taking a boat at Das-as-Wamedh Ghât, and going up the stream to Así Saugaur, thence dropping down, when the river-face of the city may be seen to great advantage. The Ghats present a picturesque appearance, crowded as they are early and late in the day with bathers of both sexes, laving their bodies in the sacred stream, and intent on the performance of the customary poojahs enjoined by their ritual. Here may be seen side by side with the coy maiden and more sedate and grave matron, the venerable priest with his young disciple, and the semi-nude ascetic with wizened aspect and withered extremities, all engaged in rites and ceremonies hallowed to them by the usages of centuries. Farther on may be observed both sexes going through their respective prostrations and perambulations before and around hideous images of clay and stone. Here, the bathers enter the water; there, they may be seen emerging and changing their light and almost transparent drapery, as if the gaze of the crowd was a matter of perfect indifference to them. It is to be presumed the bathers have faith in this cleansing process: to the more fastidious

European, it appears about the dirtiest and most indecent kind of ablution possible. Many of the Ghats on the Ganges, and especially at Benares, can lay claim to considerable architectural pretensions, although from the manner in which they are built up to and surrounded, as well as from the dilapidated condition into which they are allowed to fall, they fail to secure the attention they deserve.*

The second plan is by going on an elephant *through* the city, if the season will permit; or if the stranger prides himself on his capabilities as a pedestrian, he had better secure a guide and walk; he will thus see much more, and he will be amply repaid for the fatigue he may undergo. It is true, as it has often been observed by travellers through great cities, that the stranger will, in going through Benares, find an endless maze of streets and lanes; but let him go

* Fergusson, in his *Handbook of Architecture*, speaking on this subject, observes :—"Another object of architectural magnificence, peculiar to Northern Hindustan, is the construction of the ghats that everywhere line the river-banks in most of the great cities, more especially those which are situated on the Ganges. Benares possesses perhaps the greatest number of edifices of this class; but from Calcutta to Hurdwar no city is without some specimens of this species of architectural display."

on, and he will soon come upon some public square or chouk, where he will meet with stalls and shops of every description, from that of the seller of gold and silver brocade to the humble shed of the vendor of wooden combs and rosaries of sacred Tulsi. In one part may be seen the dealer in pearls and diamonds; in another, the artisan at his wheel, polishing the last anklet of some village beauty who is sitting by watching the operation,—the busy crowd in the meantime swaying to and fro, listlessly as would appear, but still busy in their very listlessness, a characteristic not peculiar only to the inhabitants of this great city, but applicable to all the natives of India.

The third plan, by which a stranger may have a fair view of Benares, is by ascending, in the evening, the only one of the minarets which is safe and accessible. If he be a man of nerve, he will thus be well able to see, on looking down from the highest balcony of the minaret, the whole city mapped out beneath him, and to observe the inhabitants in the inner recesses of their domiciles, attending to their domestic duties, and absorbed in the preparation of their evening meal. Having plenty of time on my hands, I chose the pedestrian tour.

As may be imagined, the principal objects of

interest, next to an inspection of the city itself, are the temples of Benares. These exist in thousands; and may be visited to a larger or smaller degree at the discretion and ability of the tourist. An inspection of a fractional part, however, even of those deemed famous by the people themselves, would be impossible and unprofitable; and I shall therefore content myself with describing the few that are of greatest note.

That most sacred to the Hindoo is the Temple of Bisheshwar, or, as it is frequently termed, the "Golden Pagoda," dedicated to the god Shiva. It is situated in a densely crowded part of the native town, and is approached through a labyrinth of "streets," or, more properly speaking, narrow paved causeways; the upper floors of the houses on each side of which frequently almost touch one another, after the fashion of some of the antiquated buildings in our old London closes and alleys.

Starting on our tour of inspection very early in the morning, in a rickety vehicle, a cross between a cab and a dak gharry, and passing the civil lines by a not unpicturesque road, we arrived in about an hour at the native quarter of the town. Here walking became necessary, and I was not sorry, in threading my way through the narrow labyrinth of its densely-thronged avenues, to have a companion by my side.

Situated in perhaps the most crowded part of the city rises, with imposing effect, this famed temple of idolatry. In structure it is a double temple of comparatively insignificant dimensions, its extreme length being only 47 feet, and greatest height 51 feet. Yet the labour and elaboration which must have been expended on its interior and exterior decoration is almost inconceivable. It stands in the midst of a covered quadrangle, and is of comparatively recent date. From the roof rise three irregular spires and domes, two of which are covered with sheet-copper gilt, presenting, as illuminated by the brilliant rays of an Eastern sun, the appearance of glittering masses of burnished gold. The cost of this gilt covering was borne by Runjeet Sing, the "Lion of the Punjab." In the vestibule, which is open above, there are four huge bells, which are almost ceaselessly rung by the worshippers with the greatest possible unction, to express their attachment and devotion to Bisheshwar.

In order to obtain a better exterior view, as

well as to escape the jostling throng, we took up a position on the roof of an opposite dwelling, and there surveyed the myriads who, in frantic eagerness, still dripping-wet from their ablutions in the holy stream, fought their way into the sacred precincts of the temple, carrying in one hand a brass vessel filled with the holy water of the Ganges, and in the other a string of yellow flowers as a votive offering, which they flung profusely about them as they entered the portals. Judging by the frantic eagerness of the crowd to approach the temple, their devotion was something more than a mere fashion; and mistaken though we know them to be in their belief, they evince a zeal in the service which we might well imitate in a better cause.

Having sated our curiosity by gazing at the still increasing throng, utterly in contrast to any English crowd, we descended from our view-point, and summoning, through the aid of a native guide, the chief Brahmin of the Pagoda as showman, we essayed an entrance into the interior of the temple itself. Preceded by half a dozen "helps," after a fearful amount of striving, pushing, and crowding, through an excited, greasy, and powerfully odorous throng of people of all ages and of both sexes—some so infirm as to be scarcely able, unassisted, to fight their way through—we reached the centre hall, in the middle of the marble floor of which, and before the *lingam* or emblem of worship, was a marble basin, into which the people were strewing their flowers, and throwing the remains of the holy water from their brass utensils. On the left-hand side of the inner recess of the temple was another similar basin, which we learnt was two feet and a half deep, and a foot and a half square at top and bottom, lined with plates of pure silver, the cost of which was defrayed by the late Peishwa, who on one occasion filled it with gold mohurs and rupees, to propitiate the divinity of the temple, as an offering for sins he had committed in a former birth, as the Brahmins maintain. When a wealthy and distinguished votary visits this shrine, the greedy and rapacious priests never fail to endeavour to impress the fact of the Peishwa's gift on his mind, for a most excellent reason, which the stranger may easily infer.

On the steps of this "holy of holies," into which none but the officiating priests and privileged worshippers are permitted to enter, we were held back, and only allowed to witness the scene from without the doorway.

The few half-clad worshippers and priests occupying this envied spot were engaged in flinging, with their hands, water and flowers from the sacred basin over the heads of the panting, striving crowd behind us, whose eagerness to gain a sight of the holy chamber and some portion of the gifts of the priests proved of no slight inconvenience to us, as, not permitted to proceed further forward, and vigorously pressed from the rear, we were in imminent danger of losing our footing altogether; the frantic throng meanwhile shouting, screaming, vociferating, howling, and making the most energetic demonstrations of zeal and religious frenzy. So overpowering was the close, almost fetid, atmosphere of the place, the smell from the oily throng, and the hideous uproar and confusion prevailing, that, nearly fainting, we gladly, but with difficulty, elbowed our way into the comparatively fresh, but still close and confined atmosphere of the street. But we were not free: a crowd of priests and mendicants followed, demanding, in no very supplicatory manner, alms and *bucksheesh;* and this we were compelled to give freely, before we could get rid of them.

The inspection of this, the great Hindoo Pagoda, is truly a task requiring an amount of courage and physical endurance not possessed by every one; but still, to obtain an adequate idea of the fanatical fervour of the deluded myriads who crowd the place, a visit is necessary; for any description of the scene must fall far short of what even the most sanguine or imaginative would picture.

The legend connected with the image now worshipped in this temple, and for the truth of which the priests are always ready to vouch, runs thus:—On the destruction of the original temple by the Mahometans, Bisheshwar himself appeared, and taking up his image leaped with it into the Gyan Bapee well to save it from pollution. Before his godship, however, had determined to take this desperate step, he condescended to appear in a dream to one of the attendant priests, and showed him what his image ought to be like for the new temple. A true and faithful representation was therefore made and set up, and the one to which the worshippers offer poojah in the modern temple is, say the priests, the veritable image made after the instructions imparted by Bisheshwar.

The natives believe that the god Shiva still resides in the Gyan Bapee—the well of knowledge; and it is still visited by multitudes, who do poojah to it, casting in sacred water and flowers as offerings and sacrifices to Shiva. I turned aside from the Golden Temple to visit the well, but was almost suffocated by the odour emitted from its putrefied contents.

There is also, some distance off, another well, even more celebrated in Hindu mythology than the last mentioned, — Mankarnika. The writer in the *Calcutta Review* before referred to thus speaks of it, and I can add nothing more descriptive or forcible:— "It is the first place sought after by the thousands of pilgrims flocking yearly to the Holy City, who are drawn towards it by a mysterious and irresistible fascination. Its fetid water is regarded as a healing balm, which will infallibly wash away all the sins of the soul and make it pure and holy. There is no sin so heinous or abominable, which, in popular estimation, it cannot instantly efface. Even for the crime of murder it can, it is said, procure forgiveness.

"A series of stone steps on each of the four sides of the well leads down to the water. The seven lowermost steps are said to be without a join, and to belong to the original well as built by divine hands; and although the singular fact of several joins being visible is, to the uninitiated, a slight difficulty in the way of such an assertion, yet the Hindus, brushing aside such a trivial circumstance, readily swallow the explanation given by the Brahmins, that the joins are only superficial and do not penetrate through the stones. Upon the stairs, in a niche on the north side, is a figure of Vishnu; and at the mouth of the well, on the west side, is a row of sixteen diminutive altars, on which pilgrims present offerings to their ancestors. The water of the well is very shallow, being not more than two or three feet in depth. It is insufferably foul, and the effluvia from it impregnate the air for some distance around. The worshipper, descending into the water, laves his head and body with the vile liquid, and at the same time utters certain phrases appointed for the ceremony."

The legend associated with this place is as absurd as it is filthy; and one can hardly credit the fact, that such monstrous and transparent fictions are believed even by the uneducated native.

There are many other noted shrines, one of the chief of which is the *Gopal Mandir*, called also *Gopal Lal ka Mandir*, sacred to Krishna. This is perhaps the richest shrine in Benares, and it enjoys a handsome income contributed by the wealthy mahajuns from all parts of India. It is situated on an elevated terrace, and has flights of steps leading up to it from the two opposite sides of the quadrangle, which the terrace represents. Here is celebrated, with great pomp and splendour, the anniversary of the birth of Krishna, and its necessary festival the Daskando. The revels and orgies connected with the celebration of these two festivals put to the blush all that one reads of in reference to the Eleusinian mysteries.

Within a walking-distance from the Golden Pagoda is a very ancient Hindu "Observatory," a very unpretending building, but possessing a peculiarly rich and elegant stone-carved balcony. It was erected by Rajah Jey Singh, of Jeypore (A.D. 1698—1742), who at one time maintained a posse of joteshes and astrologers to observe and record the motion of the sun, moon, and planets. It is now in a state of great disrepair, and the visitor is only shown a few perpendicular and horizontal dials constructed of solid masonry. The rajah had an observatory built similar in every respect, only somewhat larger, at Delhi, for the use of astrologers attached to the court of the reigning emperor. A few years ago the Jotesh in attendance showed visitors an astrolabe of brass, accurately graduated and inscribed with Hindu figures and mystical diagrams. The chief interest of this place is now its antiquity.

Proceeding from hence to an adjoining ghât of numberless slippery steps, we took our seats in a dinghy, and advanced, in this crude attempt at a "gondola," along the broad waters of the sacred Ganges, down the noble stream, in order the better to view the town from its immediate river-face.

As thus seen, the City of Benares has an imposing but marvellously strange appearance, its buildings rising one above another, amphitheatre-fashion, from the very water's edge, in a vast, complicated, and irregular mass. The river's bank is crowded with innumerable small temples occupied by hideous faqueers and priests, who are, however, only "tenants at will" of the Ganges, which in the wet monsoon rises above, and submerges, many of their shrines.

On the summit of the Madhoray Ghât, and above the mass of buildings by which it is surrounded, rises the great Mosque of Aurungzebe, built over the site of the temple of Bindo Madhub to signalize the triumph of Islam over Brahminism.

It is curious to observe how the Hindus

cherish and preserve the names of their ancient temples, &c., notwithstanding the grinding tyranny they must have endured under the bigoted rule of the Mahometans. The Hindus call the minarets of this mosque to this day "*Madho Roy ka Dharara,*" and also "*Beni Madho ka Dharara.*" Whilst the stranger may possibly sigh over the destruction of an ancient temple to make room for a more modern mosque, and accuse the Mahometan of intolerance, it would be as well for him to remember that the Hindu did not spare the Buddhist in this respect, for on this spot once stood a Buddhist Monastery, as the stones at the base of the mosque to the north, west, and south, still *in situ,* sufficiently indicate.

The minars, or towers, rise nobly 150 feet from the floor of the Musjid, which is again 80 feet above the river level. The towers have a peculiarly graceful and delicate appearance, being at the base but 8¼ feet in diameter, while at the summit this becomes again gradually reduced to 7½ feet. It may be imagined, thus, that an ascent of the minars, by its 130 winding steps, is by no means easy. It is, however, well worth the labour involved, for from the summit a wondrous view of the vast town and surrounding country and neighbourhood is obtained.

For several miles before and around lies stretched the crowded city, its gaudily-painted buildings, mostly of stone and very lofty, apparently heaped together in a tangled proximity, whilst the separating thoroughfares are hardly distinguishable from the mass, except by the sight of the busy seething crowd hurrying to and fro, and looking from this giddy height very ants in size as in number. From this lofty pinnacle, too, the bright green country is seen stretching far, far away, in a dead level plain, to the horizon.

Descending from our lofty view-point once more into the centre of the busy hive below, we threaded cautiously our way, with handkerchief to nose, out of the labyrinth, to the wider thoroughfare where our ticca gharry was in waiting; and first stopping at a toy-shop to procure some specialities of Benares ware for the *bābās* at home,* we wended our way back towards the civil lines.

One sight, however, still remained, and we

* Benares is much noted for the manufacture of wooden toys, curiously painted and varnished. The advantage of these over the ordinary description of children's toys is, that the pigment is not removable by use.

presently reached it. Situate immediately out of the native town, on the main road, is a small solid stone pagoda (the name of which I could not ascertain), enclosed in a court-yard, having a magnificent tank adjoining. The carving on the temple is most elaborate, and resembles greatly that to be seen in the Hindoo remains at Futtehpore Sikree, near Agra. Here are thousands of wild monkeys—descendants, the natives believe, of those who came to India with Hooneemàn, the Monkey-god himself. The sight of hundreds of these creatures, clustered soberly in troops just like citizens of the place, leaping and clambering about—up pillars, along roofs and parapets, chattering, gambolling, and revelling in the fullest possible civilized liberty, is a thing not easily forgotten, and constitutes, indeed, the chief attraction of the place. We gave money to purchase food, and it was a truly curious scene to witness the troop of monkeys, of every age and size, from the bearded old monster—red, black, and blue—to the tiny brown squirrel-like *bucchha*, noisily flocking from all sorts of crannies, corners, and places, at the call of the priests of the temple, each eager to receive a share, cramming their pouches with a frightened haste, as if only half assured that we meant well by them, and keeping one eye on us, either for prompt attack or retreat as occasion might serve. Many would have been ugly customers at close quarters, and seemed disposed to show fight ; but a stick half-threateningly held up was sufficient to send them scampering and swearing away. It is, however, hardly necessary to mention that the brutes are held in the highest religious estimation by the priests and people, and to strike one would lead to most serious consequences.

Some three miles distant from the city, towards the north, is a celebrated Buddhist monument, consisting of a solid round tower, some 93 feet in diameter at base, and some 110 feet high. It was built by the Buddhists, about 530 B.C., and was seen by Hwen Tsang and Fa Hiang, the two celebrated Chinese travellers, in the beginning of the 5th century A.D. Of its antiquity there is not the shadow of a doubt, and a visit to it will amply repay the stranger for the expense he may incur in gharry hire. The curious and the antiquary are referred to the descriptions furnished of it by General Cunningham, in his Archæological Survey Report.

And, lastly, there is the Sumèru Temple, at Ramnugar, on the opposite side of the river, where the Rajah of Benares usually resides. This temple is situated by the side of a large tank, which is at the distance of a mile and a half from the Rajah's palace. The lower portion of the temple, as it now appears, was built by Rajah Chet Singh, one of the predecessors of the present Rajah. The upper portion was added by the Rajah occupying the guddee, from a design prepared by the late Major Kittoe. The lower portion of this temple, and indeed the only part of it worth admiring, is covered over with exquisitely carved representations of animals in stone. Over these are images shown in the attitude of musicians playing upon the various musical instruments used by the Hindus. All these stand out in perfect relief; and though some of the figures are out of proportion, and grotesque in appearance, the carving is delicate and displays great art and skill.

The Station of Benares is notable from its being the head-quarters of the Benares Opium Agency. The poppy-growing area, under the supervision of the Benares agent, is upwards of 4,00,000 beegahs. The opium factory at Benares is well worth visiting. It is stated by a very intelligent officer of the department that, contrary to what might be expected, the health of the workmen employed in the opium factory, and in the manipulation of the drug, is not exposed to any risk whatever; whilst the impunity with which the drug is handled by hundreds of the operatives, for hours together, proves that it has no endemic action. The workmen may be seen in the large caking-vats wading knee-deep through the drug for several hours at a time, serving out the opium by armfuls, their bodies being quite naked, with the exception of a cloth about the loins. These men say they feel drowsy towards the end of the day, and declare that they are overpowered early in the evening by sleep ; but they do not complain of the effect as being either unpleasant or injurious. Some of the officers of the department are disposed to think that the soporific effect experienced by the vat-men is produced through the lungs and not through the skin.

There can be no doubt that the time is not far distant when the Government monopoly of this great opium business will be a thing of the past, and then our friends of the Celestial Empire may have to depend for the drug upon the operations of a gigantic "Great Indian Opium Company *Limited*," capital 500 crores—shares two lacs each—the share list closed—and the shares at Rs. 75,000 premium, &c. &c. &c. ! ! !

These sights seen, there is nothing to detain one in Benares, beyond a casual visit to the fine Hindoo Sanscrit College, founded in 1791; which is considered the chief seat of native learning in India.

And so, having made, this time, due *bunder-bust* with the *garrywan*, to carry me to the rail for half the sum he robbed me of in coming, I wended my way back, through the dust-bestrewn road, and over the rickety Bridge of Boats, to the homely-looking Railway Station of Benares.

CHAPTER IV.

BENARES TO ALLAHABAD.

The East-India Railway Company: its Deficient Arrangements.—The Fortress of Chunar.—Mirzapore.—The Jumna Bridge: its Size and Cost.—Sudden Rise and Fall of the River.—Allahabad.—The Fort.—The Khusru Gardens.

ENGLISHMEN are proverbially grumblers, and especially English travellers; but if ever there was cause for grumbling, I think it is on the East-India Railway. I have already spoken of the ill-arranged Railway Stations; but a more serious evil—because attended with danger — is the excessive unpunctuality prevailing. The train by which you leave Benares is timed to meet that coming up direct to the Jumna; sufficient leisure being allowed hungry travellers on arrival at Mogul Serai to get lunch or a meal. More often than not, however, if coming from Benares, you might have a meal and forty winks too, since the trains are seldom more punctual than an hour or two *late.* And then the dusty carriages! It is bad enough, after a long journey, to find the pores of your skin clogged with dirt, which, glutenized by perspiration, causes you to feel as if gummed all over; but, freshly washed and brushed, to step into a carriage coated with the dust of some hundreds of miles of Indian travel, is a step beyond the reasonable limit of patient endurance. To my simple understanding, it seemed quite practicable thoroughly to cleanse the carriages at every principal junction—the first-class ones at any rate; and highly necessary is it to do so. I can truly say, however, that not once was this adequately done intermediately from Calcutta to Delhi; and beyond putting in the lamps at night (which invariably went out an hour after), the employés of the railway seemed to disturb themselves little with attending to the train.

The route onwards to Allahabad presents in some respects a marked change to the country left behind. The ground is still painfully flat, but there is a dryness noticeable in the air, not experienced before; the grass, too, is browner, and corn, pulse, and mustard take the place of the marsh lands and the bright green paddy so constantly seen in Lower Bengal. *En route* is passed the fine fortress of Chunar, picturesquely situated on a rocky eminence, used by Government formerly as a state prison, and around which many military pensioners are quartered. Then Mirzapore, not inaptly termed the Birmingham of India: and so we arrive at the Jumna Bridge Station, separated only by the Jumna river (about $\frac{3}{4}$ of a mile wide at this spot) from the Allahabad shore. A handsome structure now connects the Bengal Rail with the North-Western Province line. The bridge is of iron girders on stone piers, which are 62 feet in height from the low-water level, with foundations 24 feet again below this level. The roadway is 3,184 feet long, having at present but one line of rails laid. The cost of this notable structure was £385,000. At the time I passed, the bridge was incomplete, and it was a most wearisome task waiting to be ferried over in the steam-barge. Besides this, the passengers were kept no less than three hours on the Allahabad side, under a temporary shed, before the train took us to the Allahabad Station, only three miles distant. Here, as elsewhere on the Indian lines, supervision seems to be sadly needed.

The appearance of the Jumna even in the dry season struck me as very imposing; with its enormous span from shore to shore, shut in by high shelving sandy banks—its then placid waters a clear bright blue; but what must be the effect in the freshes, when its surging waters rush resistlessly past in a creamy whirl, and its banks are hidden by a suddenly-formed expanse of water more resembling sea than river!

The rivers in India, for the most part, indeed, are subject to extraordinary variations of rise and fall in the different monsoons. During this year the Jumna, with a velocity of nine miles an hour, rose at this spot in three days to a height of 36 feet above low-water mark, and was within a few inches of submerging the then only unfinished pier of the railway bridge. Fortunately, however, the water subsided as rapidly as it rose, and the brickwork of the pier was safely proceeded with. But for interruptions of this kind it would long since have been completed. A like difficulty was experienced with the Saône railway bridge, the piers of which were carried away a countless number of times by the rushing torrent, which in the dry season dwindles away to a mere rivulet.

Arrived at Allahabad, you have the choice of a host of very passable hotels; and in view to seeing the place, you of course hire a vehicle, for Allahabad is one of the most straggling of places. A new town is, however, in course of formation, and must soon become of importance, Allahabad being now the seat of Government of the North-Western Provinces.

The roads of the city are remarkably good, but terribly dusty, and the glare is intense. This latter is probably attributable to the paucity of trees and shrubs in the place. The very grass has a withered and dusty appearance, and nothing will grow unless copiously watered by means of canals filled from wells, the water being raised toilsomely by bullocks. The process, crude and tedious as it is, seems very effective, and is the only means of irrigation pursued in producing the crops of the surrounding country. Were one solely in search of the picturesque or marvellous, it is not to Allahabad one should go to find it. There are, nevertheless, some objects of considerable interest in the place, the principal of which are the Fort and the Khusru Gardens. The fort was built by Akbar, and is memorable in our time as having sheltered the European troops and residents during the mutiny. It is a striking place of great extent, being 2,500 yards in circuit, and once held, if it does not at present, the largest arsenal in India. The principal gate is surmounted by a dome with a wide hall beneath, surrounded by arcades and galleries, and ornamented with paintings in relief. The structure is said to have cost £1,750,000, but since the time of its erection it has been considerably altered and improved to suit the necessities of modern warfare. In the middle of the fort "stands an antique stone column, popularly styled *Gada,* or Club of Bhim Sen, a hero who figures in the romantic legends of Hindostan. It is mentioned by Tieffenthaler as standing in his time, was pulled down during some alterations made in the fort in 1798, and has lately been replaced. The length is forty-two feet seven inches; the shape nearly cylindrical, yet slightly tapering; the lower diameter being three feet two and a quarter inches; the upper two feet two inches. It bears two Sanskrit inscriptions of considerable length, and obviously of remote antiquity; but, notwithstanding the endeavours of Prinsep, Troyer, and Mill, no certain conclusion can be drawn as to their date."* In the fort is a curious subterranean passage, the native account of which is, that it runs to Brindabum (Benares). I was only able to proceed, however, some fifty yards into the place, owing to the confined atmosphere putting out the light; but those who have proceeded further say that a tamarind tree grows there! Close to the fort walls is the actual confluence of the Ganges and the Jumna —Allahabad being thus situate at the *embouchure* of these two mighty rivers, a spot held particularly sacred by Hindoos, and visited yearly, it is said, by 200,000 pilgrims.

Allahabad appears to have been a very favourite residence of Shah Jehan, and the fort was celebrated for its wondrous pavilion, the Chalīs Sitoon, or Hall of Forty Pillars. When material was required for the repair of the fort, the pavilion was barbarously removed; and the great hall, now used as an arsenal, alone remains,—but so plastered over, bricked up, and deformed, that it is difficult to realize in it the beautiful structure it was known once to have been.

* Thornton's *Gazetteer of India.*

The Khusru Gardens adjoin the railway station on the right, and are thus described by Thornton :—" Among the finest structures of Allahabad is that called the Serai of Khusru, the ill-fated son of Jehangir.* It is a fine quadrangle, surrounded by an embattled wall, along the inside of which are a series of lodges for the gratuitous reception of travellers. Adjoining is a garden or pleasure-ground, containing some fine old mango-trees, and three mausoleums, in a rich, magnificent, yet solemn style of architecture. Heber states that they were raised over two princes and a princess of the imperial family, but does not specify their names."

It was in these gardens that the Moulvee head of the rebellion held his court during the memorable events at Allahabad, in 1857. They now serve as an agreeable place of retreat in the cool of the morning and evening; and are tastefully arranged and cultivated, having a very pretty but not over intricate "maze." An extremely fine view is obtainable from the high terrace-roofs of the mausoleums, which are

* Khusru was the eldest son of Jehangir, and had his eyes put out by his father's orders for repeated rebellions. He was afterwards assassinated through the instrumentality of his brother, Shah Jehan.

approached by curiously-built stone staircases in the solid wall.

Next to their mosques, the Mussulman conquerors of India seem to have delighted to lavish wealth upon their tombs. Indeed, a high authority has well remarked, that the tombs of the Turks and Moguls form a complete and unbroken series of architectural monuments from the first years of the Moslem invasion to the present hour. True it is, that in no country in the world do we meet with such wondrously beautiful sepulchres in such an enduring state of preservation. Their builders must have only too faithfully followed the wishes of their founders in creating works calculated to last for all time; whilst the designs, coming down to us as they do through the lapse of centuries, show too well how much we have yet to learn before we can ever attempt successfully to imitate the magnificence and exquisite beauty found in the tombs and palaces of the kings and nobles of the Mahometan era. Many of these, far more remarkable than the mausoleums in the Serai of Khusru, I shall have occasion hereafter to refer to and describe fully.

Allahabad I found very cool in the early part of February, but from the latter end of March to the commencement of the rains, during which interval the hot winds blow, the sun is intensely powerful. The ground, too, becomes parched, and cracks in deep fissures; while the wind, blowing over the arid heated plain, shrivels up the herbage. All nature seems to faint and gasp under the scorching glow; and it is marvellous that the thirsty kine find sufficient pasturage. It can be well imagined, then, how grateful in the hot season is the Indian bungalow, with its thick grass roof, its stone or cement flooring covered with clean, cool matting, and its massive, whitewashed walls, resisting the fiery glow without; while fronting the entrances are the cooling, sweet-scented khus-khus screens, through which the hot air rushes in grateful perfumed coolness.

Allahabad is not now, as formerly, mainly occupied by civil and military functionaries, but has a large and extending trading community. There are, besides, a great many bungalows and barracks occupied by the large staff pertaining to the railway company, whose premises here cover several acres of ground; for, as the terminus of the North-Western Province line, Allahabad is necessarily a most important station of the East-Indian Railway. And now that through-communication is established between Calcutta and Delhi, a few years hence will doubtless see Allahabad a highly flourishing and extensive city.

Beyond the places of interest I have described there is little of note in Allahabad, and it is that sort of place one would not stay longer in than could be helped. Now, by means of the rail, you are within six hours' journey of Cawnpore. What saving of blood and treasure would not have been effected, had such been the case in 1857! Indeed, it is hardly too much to say that, had our railway and telegraphic communication existed then as it now does, a mutiny of the wide-spread and powerful organization which that of 1857 assumed would not have been possible.

CHAPTER V.

CAWNPORE TO LUCKNOW.

Cawnpore: as it was and as it is.—Up-country Hotels.—The Memorial Garden.—The Grave-yard: "Fairy Rings."— Wheeler's Entrenchment.—The Ambush.—Dâk Gharries.—Dâk *Tats:* Their Treatment.—The Alumbagh.—Havelock's Tomb.—The Dâk Bungalow.

CAWNPORE, ever memorable as the scene of the most barbarous act of the Mutiny of 1857, is situated on the right bank of the Ganges, and was once a place of considerable importance and busy traffic. Skinner thus describes the appearance of the river in his time:—"Every description of vessel that can be imagined was collected along the bank: the pinnaçe, which, with its three masts and neat rigging, might have passed for a ship; budgerows— the clumsiest of all clumsy things—with their sterns several times higher than their bows; and beauleahs, ugly enough, but lightly skimming along like gondolas, compared with the heavy craft about them; the drifting haystacks, which the country boats appear to be when at a distance, with their native crews, straining every nerve, upon their summits, and cheering themselves with a wild and not unfrequently a sweet song; panchways shooting swiftly down the stream, with one person only on board, who sits at the head steering with his right hand, rowing with his foot, and in the left hand holding his pipe. A ferry-boat constantly plying across the stream adds to the variety of the scene, by its motley collection of passengers—travellers, merchants, and faquirs, camels, bullocks, and horses, all crowded together. The vessels fastened to the shore are so closely packed, that they appeared to me one mass, and from their thatched roofs and low entrances might easily pass for a floating village."

Nothing of the kind is now to be seen, however, and whatever it might once have been, it is now one of the most wretchedly dismal of halting places :—a dirty and forsaken river; a dusty, barren, withered plain; an atmosphere of dust; ranges of gloomy-looking barracks and store-houses, and a few dreary-looking bungalows here and there. And yet, even so recently as the period just before the Mutiny, Cawnpore was considered a gay place, and had two cavalry regiments, two batteries of artillery, and three regiments of infantry stationed there. This it will probably never be again; and beyond the necessity of its retention, in a military point of view, for the sake of its position as the high road to Oude, there is nothing, apart from the drawback of its associations, likely to restore to it the importance it once held when Oude was in possession of an almost independent native government, and Cawnpore was considered as a frontier line, on this side, to British possessions.

The native town is long and straggling, stretching east and west, with a well-built canal and locks intersecting it north by south. The civil station is a most inconvenient distance from the railway, lying about three miles to the west. The cantonments and barracks are on a large open plain to the east, and the plan of the city altogether seems adapted to produce the highest possible discomfort and inconvenience. The remains of a once strong fort, composed of earth-work, supported by masonry, stand on the banks of the Jumna, but will not repay the trouble of inspection.

There were only two hotels in the place at the time of my visit, but a third has since been opened. The best then was the railway hotel, kept by a Mr. Jacobs: a curious anomaly of tinsel and gingerbread decorations it presented internally; but the charges were moderate and the fare, for an Indian Up-country "hotel," passable. Indeed, it is time that I should disenchant the reader of any too extravagant ideas he may have formed as to the comforts of hotels in the Upper Provinces of India. Commencing with Allahabad (where they do not always allow you musquito curtains, although there are plenty of mosquitoes), a change of a woeful nature is seen when contrasted with the comparatively luxurious hotels of Calcutta, much abused even as *they* are. Bare, cheerless rooms, with scanty furniture, and that of the poorest; no bed; ill-fitting doors and windows which neither open nor shut properly; bad food and dirty Khitmutgars; high charges and no attention—this, as to Up-country hotels, is the rule. Some are better than the rest, but my own experience is that all are bad if we think what they should and might be. Possibly, as more travellers pass and repass, in time some enterprising individual will awake to the advantage of paying a little more regard to the comfort of his visitors, and not leave them absolutely at the mercy of his Khansamah, as is almost now the invariable rule, the "landlord," whom you rarely see, appearing to do little more than make out the bill —which you need closely examine ere you pay.

It is at the hotels after leaving Allahabad that you begin to experience, in the early part of the year, the full advantage of your *resai*, pillow, and railway rug. The article given you to sleep on, dignified with the name of a bedstead, is nothing more than a charpoy—a frame-work of four bamboos on as many stumpy legs half a foot from the ground. The bottom of the bed is made by very coarse linen bands plaited athwart and across. When I asked for a mattress, sheets, and pillows, the bearer stared at me with astonishment.

"*Hum isā kistere soeega?*"—"How can I sleep like this?" said I.

"*Huzoor, sub sahib loq isā sota hy.*"—"All the gentlemen sleep like this, your honour."

"Then," thought I, "they must have been hard sleepers."

I succeeded, however, with difficulty in getting a sheet, which ordinarily did duty as a table-cloth; but for the rest of the bedding accompaniments, they were not. I had originally started unprovided with any of these essentials, but, most fortunately, had, on the road, been warned to procure them. I thus escaped an otherwise almost certain rheumatism.

Notwithstanding the scant attention you get

at these places, on leaving you find a small crowd of people at the door soliciting presents. These generally consist of the Khansamah, his assistant Khitmutgar, the Musalchee, the bearer and his "mate," the Bheestie, the Mehther, the cooly who has, uninvited, lifted your luggage to the top of the gharry, and the syce and coachman who are about to drive you to the rail. At first I gave to all, each seeming to have equal claims—*i. e.* none having *any*, as you pay handsomely for all in the hotel charges. I got rid this way of a good many rupees, until an old civilian, whom I subsequently met and journeyed with for many days, assured me I should find more thanks if I gave less, and more satisfaction still if I gave nothing. I altered my plan afterwards, only giving the servants presents when they really went out of their way to be attentive—which was very seldom; and I found the result to be that the natives looked on me with greater real respect, if not admiration.

Englishmen in India, as a rule, are not merely satisfied with giving, but they give so disproportionately as entirely to destroy the impression they wish to create: the consequence is, that now a native cannot be *looked at* without asking for *bucksheesh*, and is insolent if you do not give him forty times his desert. Two annas (3*d.*) to a Khitmutgar in receipt of seven rupees a month is, to him, what 1*s.* 6*d.* would be to a London waiter; whilst the same amount to a cooly, or menial servant, is equivalent to one day's wages. And yet I have frequently seen one rupee given to a Khitmutgar, and four annas to a cooly, when, had the proper amount been awarded, two annas to the one, and one pice to the other, would have been adequate remuneration, supposing any at all to have been deserved, and, further, would have fully satisfied them. Were *bucksheesh* given only when deserved, travellers would soon find a marked improvement in the behaviour and attention of native servants on the road, as there is no man who will cringe lower or show more obsequiousness, if there is anything to be made by it, than a native menial.

But to resume. Once lodged in your hotel, the first operation after arrival is to indulge in the luxury of a bath, and arrange for a vehicle to convey you to the objects of interest in Cawnpore. These consist of the "Well," the site of the "Slaughter-house" adjoining, Wheeler's Entrenchments, and the spot on the river's bank, whence the guns planted in ambush destroyed so many of the refugees when they took to the boats.

A short drive along a frightfully dusty road (Cawnpore seems made of dust) takes you to the Memorial Garden—now a pretty green spot, neatly enclosed, comprising the space on which the "Slaughter-house" and the "Well" stood. At the entrance-gates you are stopped by the guard, and requested to *walk* your horse along the broad gravelled paths, the propriety of which you at once recognize.

Fronting you, on a raised mound, stands the Memorial erected over the spot where lie the victims of that foulest deed of history perpetrated by order of the arch-fiend, the Nana.*

* It may not be uninteresting here to append the vivid account of the last scene of this tragedy recorded in Mr. Trevelyan's "Story of Cawnpore:"—"The sepoys were bidden to fall on. Half-a-dozen among them advanced, and discharged their muskets through the windows at the ceiling of the apartments. Thereupon the five men entered. It was the short gloaming of Hindostan—the hour when ladies take their evening-drive. Shrieks and scuffling acquainted those without that the journeymen were earning their hire. Survur Khan soon emerged with his sword broken off at the hilt. He procured another from the Nana's house, and a few minutes after appeared again on the same errand. The third blade was of better temper; or perhaps the thick of the work was already over. By the time darkness had closed in, the men came forth, and locked up the house for the night. Then the screams ceased; but the groans lasted

Annexed is an illustration of the Memorial, copied from a photograph taken on the spot. The style, it will be seen, is plain and severe, but elegant and appropriate to its object. It is difficult to read its inscription, telling of

till morning. The sun rose as usual. When he had been up nearly three hours, the five repaired to the scene of their labours over-night. They were attended by a few sweepers, who proceeded to transfer the contents of the house to a dry well situated behind some trees which grew hard by. 'The bodies,' says one who was present throughout, 'were dragged out, most of them by the hair of the head. Those who had clothes worth taking were stripped. Some of the women were alive. I cannot say how many; but three could speak. They prayed for the sake of God that an end might be put to their sufferings. I remarked one very stout woman, a half-caste, who was severely wounded in both arms, who entreated to be killed. She and two or three others were placed against the bank of the cut by which bullocks go down in drawing water. The dead were first thrown in. Yes, there was a great crowd looking on; they were standing along the walls of the compound. They were principally city people and villagers. Yes, there were also sepoys. Three boys were alive. They were fair children. The eldest, I think, must have been six or seven, and the youngest five years. They were running round the well (where else could they go to?), and there was none to save them. No; none said a word, or tried to save them. At length the smallest of them made an infantile attempt to get away. The little thing had been frightened past bearing by the murder of one of the surviving ladies. He thus attracted the observation of a native, who flung him and his companions down the well.' One deponent is of opinion that the man first took the trouble to kill the children. Others

CAWNPORE MEMORIAL

those cruelly-slaughtered Christian women and children whose gashed remains lie entombed in the well beneath, without deep emotion. And a recollection of its origin sends the blood shuddering back to the heart, and, spite of Christian charity, still awakes feelings of angry vengeance against the miscreants who, lost to a sense of the commonest humanity, perpetrated a deed at which their countrymen should for ever, but I regret to say do not, blush.

Strange to say, great as have been the blessings of our rule to all classes in India, there seems little, if any, appreciation by the natives themselves of the manifold advantages they enjoy in this respect; and I verily believe a majority of the population, if permitted the choice, would return to the old system of Mussulman domination. It is difficult to account for this except upon the supposition that our

think not. The corpses of the gentlemen must have been committed to the same receptacle; for a townsman who looked over the brink fancied that there was 'a Sahib uppermost.' This is the history of what took place at Cawnpore, between four in the afternoon of one day and nine in the morning of another, almost under the shadow of the Church tower and within call of the Theatre, the Assembly Rooms, and the Masonic Lodge. Long before noon on the 16th of July there remained no living European within the circuit of the station."

rule interferes with a brutal abandonment to the worst features of their religion; tolerant as we are in a general sense. The brutish and degrading customs of the Hindoo religion, which our Government has found it essential at different times to suppress, held, and still hold, no inconsiderable sway over the minds of an uneducated and desperately bigoted people. The Mussulman conquerors were wise in their generation in the matter of religious rule; for though claiming for themselves and for their faith absolute power and prominence, they yet permitted the freest liberty to their Hindoo subjects, whose temples and endowments became as sacredly respected as their own.

The mutiny of 1857 showed us too clearly the small hold we possessed in the affections of the people, to cause us to place a blind reliance on them again. But if we are ever to make the country great, we must continue in the civilizing policy we have begun; and while respecting the legitimate exercise of religions antagonistic to our own, we must repress with the strong hand debasing practices, the demoralizing influences of which are calculated to undo our good work of enlightening and regenerating the rising generation of the natives of India.

The Cawnpore Memorial stands, as will be seen from my illustration, in the midst of a large enclosure, which has been tastefully laid out as a garden and shrubbery.

No native is permitted to enter here without a permit from the authorities, and it is right that it should be so; for the European in charge of the grounds informed me that on two occasions he had to turn "respectable" natives out of the enclosure for grossly disrespectful conduct and deliberate levity in this sacred spot, directed, he assured me, at the Memorial itself. I sympathized with the honest man's indignation, as, with flushed cheek, he told me he had not over-gently ejected them from the place.

The graveyard is here close by, where many a gallant fellow as well as hapless woman and tender infant repose. Some few very appropriate monuments have been erected to the memory of the slain by brother officers and soldiers; but the many little grass-covered mounds are, in their simplicity, more eloquent than even marble urn or graven epitaph. The keeper of the place, pointing to some patches of ground where the grass but feebly sprouted forth, and which somewhat resembled the "fairy rings" one sees sometimes in country spots, said—"These are the places, Sir, where the little children lie buried. The grass won't grow here, water it ever so much." I replied—"Are you really in earnest?" He said—"On my word, Sir, I have these places watered twice a day, and no grass will grow; and it seems to me like a curse of God on the spot and for the men as did it." Without going so far as to endorse the conclusion sought to be arrived at, I have every belief that the man spoke the truth, as to the bare *fact*, in simple faith.

At the time of my visit, a memorial statue was lying unpacked in boxes on the ground, some difference of opinion having arisen as to the appropriate manner and place of its erection. I hope it may, ere this work is published, have found a fitting resting-place.

I left the spot with mingled feelings of regret and thankfulness—regret that the deed had been so feebly avenged, but thankfulness that it still pleased God to bless our arms, and spread the fear of our name amongst a people who, had they but half the courage that they have duplicity and wickedness, would long since have driven us from the land.

Close to the present barracks, next to Wheeler's entrenchments, or rather the locality of these (for the entrenchments themselves have been long since levelled), a monument marks the spot where hundreds of our brave soldiers and residents of the place were buried "where they fell." Looking at the extent of the ground said to have been enclosed, one wonders how General Wheeler could have hoped, with the handful of men he then had, to defend so inaccessible a place, and why he did not select much safer shelter. But conjecture at this distance of time, even were it just or appropriate, would be useless. Enough to know that he and all with him nobly maintained by their courage the reputation the British soldier has ever held.

Returning towards the Memorial Garden, and a few hundred yards distant from it, is the site of the Hindoo Temple, on the banks of the river, where a cannon in ambush was posted by the Nana, which in great part destroyed the fugitives who had received permission, under truce, to take to the boats.

Of these, but two, I believe, succeeded in escaping. Of those who were captured or found alive, some were butchered on the spot, while the rest were carried back to the "slaughter-house," to endure their still more horrible fate.

It seems to be part of the organization of the

black, that the blood once roused, he is capable of the most atrocious cruelty. This was not simply a massacre by a low and brutal mob, but the leader and his counsellors were men of position and education, who were in the habit of mingling and exchanging all the courtesies of life with those whom they doomed to such foul slaughter.

The friend of the black will tell you, at Exeter Hall, that he is your equal, and deserves to be treated as such. Putting aside the fact, that these sensation orators speak of their subject mostly from no larger an acquaintance than a missionary report affords, I may say, from an experience of many years amongst the natives of India, that they are not and probably never will be the equals of Europeans in that country; and that any legislation which seeks to treat them as such, must bear unjustly on the European. How can one deem as equals a class swayed by no moral perceptions, fearing no divine retribution, and with whom falsehood is more familiar than truth. When the superstitions and the debasing effects of immoral and idolatrous religions shall be supplanted by strict adherence to a belief in a moral, if not divine, law, then the natives of India may, with a better grace, demand to be considered the equals of the now dominant race; for in this advance they will have shown themselves to be possessed of a sterling power of self-development, and to be animated by the noblest of ambitions.

The reader will, perhaps, prefer that I should abandon moralizing, and revert to adventure. Returning, then, to the hotel, I now made arrangements for a dâk to Lucknow, being unable to resist the temptation of paying a visit to this notable city, the capital of the vast province of Oude. The N. W. Dâk Company provides a dâk gharry to Lucknow for ten rupees, with an extra charge of five rupees for each additional person. Besides this, there is a toll of one rupee per head to pay for crossing the bridge of boats to the Lucknow shore from Cawnpore; and a more rickety, old-fashioned method of crossing a river, in this enlightened and progressive nineteenth century, cannot well be imagined :—a lot of ill-shaped country barges moored together, covered with planks, and the surface overlaid with straw and earth; as uneven and, apparently, unsafe a platform as anything can well be.* There is nothing what-

* A pontoon bridge is in course of construction to replace the bridge of boats. The work, I was informed, is being

ever to prevent your being precipitated off the bridge into the river, were the oxen so disposed; and such a catastrophe is at times by no means improbable, as the usually patient cattle, made obstinate by over-work and ill-treatment, frequently back and edge off in a manner highly unsatisfactory to a nervous person. Approaching the entrance to the bridge, down a steep and horribly dusty incline, full of pitfalls in the shape of deep ruts, your horse is taken out of the gharry, and a couple of strong oxen yoked to it, who painfully and slowly drag you across the creaking, shaky, jolting platform. Ultimately, to your extreme thankfulness, you are landed on the opposite bank, where, having, if you be wise, refused the application of the lazy bullock-driver for *bucksheesh*, your horse is re-harnessed, and you commence your journey, probably for the first time, in a "dâk gharry."

Whether it be that the more rapid and easy locomotion of the Rail has spoilt the present

executed by contract on the following terms: the contractor is to receive the tolls for ten years, commencing with the date of present contract; and, on completion of the pontoon bridge, Government are to purchase it from the contractor at cost price; the latter engaging to keep in repair the old bridge, at his own cost, till the new one is completed.

generation for dâk travelling, or whether the latter always was as it now is and seems likely to remain, I do not know; but anything more uncomfortable, more barbarous, or more inhuman than dâk travelling on the Grand Trunk Road, I have never witnessed, and hope never to witness. At starting from Cawnpore, a tolerably decent but decidedly careworn steed was harnessed to our vehicle—a rather large and strongly built gharry, which bore evidence of having once upon a time been painted green. An outer canvass sunshade hung on either side; while inside a rickety shelf served for placing loose articles upon: from the roof hung a considerably worn and "holy" piece of network, designed to hold your nightcap or the like; while a couple of cracked planks, stretching from seat to seat, and covered with faded cushions, were explained as intended to do duty for a bed. Is this, thought I, the "comfortable dâk gharry" we so often hear old Indians talk of, while bewailing its displacement by the Rail? My second reflection was, how were two of us possibly to make ourselves snug, for a forty-six miles' journey, in this miserable box. As I looked at it—now already half-filled with bags and parcels, blankets and pillows—visions of dislocated bones, cramped limbs, and soured temper, flashed across me; and I felt that if my travelling companion and I arrived at Lucknow without quarrelling, we must be the most amiable of mortals. However, there was no help for it; and as nobody seemed inclined to commiserate us, in we tumbled.

Soon after leaving the bridge of boats, our coachman pulled up, and commenced changing horses. Well, thought I, if this is the length of stage, we shall do well. Toò soon, however, I discovered the object of this humanity. Our first steed was the "show" horse, with which to start from the Station. Our next, and the ones following, over a journey of forty-six miles—how shall I describe them? Wretched, half-starved tats,* with every good principle they ever inherited destroyed; rendered vicious by a lifetime of starvation and ill-treatment; scarcely able to drag *themselves* along, much less a heavy, well-laden vehicle—no wonder that, with instinctive knowledge, they put their shoulders to the wheel (*i. e.* backed) instead of to the collar, and resolutely declined to proceed. At length, goaded by the lashes of a coachman on one side, and by the thrusts

* A tat is a country-bred pony.

and blows from a syce on the other, assisted by a steady push at the wheels from some half-dozen attendant nature-clad "grooms," our poor beast leaped off, to pull up again so soon as the first impulse was over; and only to be set in motion once more by a renewal of the humane treatment first adopted, or by the coachman or syce, or both, running alongside and plying it with blows thick and fast the while. Willingly would I have walked the whole way had such been possible:—as it was, I essayed one stage, but was obliged to give in. On remonstrating vigorously with the coachman, to whom I felt much inclined to apply a little of the same discipline wherewith he had treated his unfortunate horse, he said (commencing with the usual native reply — "*Hum kea kurrega?*—What can I do?")—"The horses have had no food (corn) for two months, the sircar not having given us any money."

The fact is undeniable that it is only by blows and scourgings that the poor beasts can be got to do the work for which they are physically unfit, being fed apparently only upon grass, and frequently covered with hideous sores from ill-treatment and ill-fitting harness. It is no uncommon thing for a horse to be made to do two stages running, because of the break-down of a neighbouring gharry: so that if the horses have any stamina in them, they are soon ruined by over-work.

To make matters worse, one set of harness (save the mark !) is made to do for horses of all shapes and sizes, so that the sore backs and galled necks the poor brutes commonly suffer under are easily accounted for. I should scarcely have believed it possible that a public company, or even a private owner, could knowingly carry on a traffic in so inhuman a manner; and yet all the horses on the line belonging to the various companies running, both here and elsewhere on my route, were the same, and subjected to the same treatment; and I am told it is more or less so all over India. Truly it is time that the iron horse should take the place of these dwarfed and ill-used specimens of the brute creation, and such, it is to be hoped, will ere long be the case. On my arrival at Lucknow, a distance of forty-six miles from Cawnpore (which occupied *eleven hours*, without stopping), I wrote to the agent, who expressed surprise and regret at what I related. And doubtless he was perfectly blameless; but some one is surely responsible: and it behoves the authorities to interfere and put a stop to brutality which would, in a more civilized country, be severely dealt with.*

The state of things described is the less excusable, as in this distance of forty-six miles there are no less than eight changes of horses; but, of course, what avails the changes, if tired cattle, "fresh" from one stage, are used for the relay? Travellers cannot do much, but they can do something to remove the evil,—complain without ceasing; and in no case should they fee the coachman if a bad horse has been put in during his stage.

It being night when I arrived at Lucknow, I did not perceive the first place of interest which presented itself at the Lucknow end of the Cawnpore Road—the famous Alumbagh; but on my return I stopped at and examined it. It was formerly a garden-house of the King of Oude, and comprises a walled enclosure of 500 square yards. The house itself is an unpretending square building of two stories, having a turret at each corner. The garden was once well stocked with fruit-trees and ornamental shrubs, but it now presents a most desolate

* The evil complained of has reached such a climax that the authorities have, to some extent, now interfered, which they ought to have done long ago, and yet to do still further.

aspect. The building, too, is battered with shot and shell, and the wall destroyed in many parts.

At the commencement of the siege of the Residency, the Alumbagh was held by the mutineers; but on the third and successful advance of Outram and Havelock, from the 23rd to the 26th of September, the rebels were driven out, and the place fully occupied by our troops. Havelock and Outram made this their head-quarters before essaying the relief of the "illustrious garrison." It was here that Outram was left by Sir Colin Campbell to hold the city in check while he went to settle accounts with the Gwalior Contingent. It had been the intention of Havelock, after effecting the relief of the Residency, to retire on the Alumbagh, and so protect the withdrawal of the relieved garrison on their road to Cawnpore. With this view, in his third and successful advance, the army-baggage and tents were left at the Alumbagh under a guard of 530 infantry and several guns. The evacuation of the Residency was found impossible, however, in consequence of inability to procure transport for the sick, wounded, and women and children, and from the fact that the only road of escape was still in many parts completely under the enemy's fire.* The Alumbagh remained, therefore, in the hands of this small protecting force, exposed to repeated attacks from the enemy, until the advance of Sir Colin Campbell in the early part of November. This position, as the key to the base at Cawnpore, proved of infinite service; and it was also useful as a means of communication with the beleagured garrison of the Residency, between which and the Alumbagh force, despite the harassing fire of the enemy, semaphore signals † were constantly exchanged.

In the garden of the Alumbagh is Sir Henry Havelock's tomb — Havelock, the Christian soldier, who was "cut down by disease in the moment of his greatest triumph, in the noontide of his glory, before envy had time to dim his laurels, or malice to tarnish his renown." No one should visit Lucknow without staying

* An idea of the difficulty of the position may be formed from the fact that the small relieving force, in cutting its way through to the Residency, lost 535 men, killed, wounded, and missing; the brave General Neil being one of the former.

† The following significant passage occurs in Mr. Gubbins's diary during the siege: — "November 12. . . . . The enemy do not seem to know the meaning of the working of the long arms of the machine, but, observing the figures occasionally on the roof, have opened a smart fire of musketry upon it."

to drop a tear over the resting-place of the good Havelock. As long as the memory of great deeds, high courage, and spotless devotion is cherished among his countrymen, so long will Havelock's lonely tomb in the grave beneath the scorching Eastern sky, hard by the vast city, the scene alike of his toil, his triumph, and his death, be regarded as one of the most holy of the many spots where our patriot soldiers lie. He died (24th November) from dysentery at the Dilkooshah, on the relief and evacuation of Lucknow by Sir Colin Campbell, on the very day, it is said, that the last of the besieged had evacuated the Baillie Guard in safety. He lived thus to see the consummation of his hopes, and was buried within sight of the place where he fought so nobly and so long. Though all that is mortal of the brave soldier lies beneath the spot where now the marble stone attests his deeds, these live still freshly in the hearts of his countrymen near and far away.

The Alumbagh also is noted as the first place of shelter afforded to the relieved garrison on their memorable retirement with Sir Colin's force to Cawnpore, on November 27, 1857.

Most travellers make the journey from Cawnpore to Lucknow by night, it being far less tedious, and the road presenting absolutely nothing of interest. A visit to the Alumbagh, however, can be more satisfactorily made from Lucknow, the distance being only some three miles, and making a pleasant trip before breakfast.

There are but two hotels in Lucknow: one at the entrance of the town, and the other near Wingfield Park. There was also till recently a capital dâk bungalow; but the municipal authorities have done away with it, *at the request of the hotel proprietors!* For the sake of travellers this is greatly to be regretted; for it makes still more independent a class who were, previously even, by no means sufficiently alive to their responsibilities.

True, the dâk bungalow, as at present conducted, hardly meets the wants of the *luxurious* traveller. Situate, as a rule, in as desolately-chosen a spot as possible—its almost bare rooms suggestive of an equally impoverished *cuisine*—its travellers' book abounding probably with the lamentations of departed guests, the *tout ensemble* is no more calculated to give one an appetite, than is the leathery steak, or sinewy bantam you erewhile saw sporting about the "compound," calculated to satisfy it. Yet these dâk bungalows were not bad things in their way in the olden time, when, from paucity of travellers, no other halting-places for refreshment existed. The mistake is that, if they are kept up at all, they should be so ill-provided as but to half serve the purpose. It is quite possible that, in a pecuniary sense, they do not pay: they are, nevertheless, in many parts of the country an absolute necessity; and it would surely be better to increase the rate, if the charge of one rupee per day per head, for the privilege of sleeping on a charpoy, be not sufficient, rather than to maintain such desirable conveniences in so unsuitable a manner. One great recommendation with many is, that the dâk bungalow is cheap; for though the old villain of an attendant khansamah mulcts you pretty handsomely for the fare he supplies you with, as the range of choice of provisions is limited to the smallest possible variety, you cannot be *very* extravagant. By the rules, no traveller is permitted to occupy a room in the bungalow more than twenty-four hours if another in-coming traveller requires it; but I have known "old stagers," on economy bent, take up their quarters in the bungalow for days together, refusing to budge. It is satisfactory to know that *some* are satisfied.

CHAPTER VI.

LUCKNOW.

Lucknow: its Origin; Purity of the Atmosphere; Cleanliness of the Station; Demeanour of the Natives; its Hospitals and Charities; its prominent Buildings; special Events of the Mutiny; Culture of the Silk-worm. — Icefields. — The Chowk: an Elephant-ride through it.

LUCKNOW, the capital of the territory of Oude, is situate on the right, or south-western, side of the River Goomtee. It derives its name from Luchmanpore, and Liknow, once two very large and important villages, or from one Lickna, an architect, who built a fort on the site of the present Muchee Bhawun, and the place first claimed to be the capital of Oude eighty or a hundred years ago, on the accession of Asf-o-Dowla. Of the mass of buildings which, facing inwards, extend from the river bank (vast portions having been cleared away since the Mutiny), the middle part, considered to have formed the ancient city, was founded by Lakshmuna, brother of Rama.

Thornton, speaking of Lucknow, says:—"According to tradition, the stronghold of Lucknow was on an eminence, and was demolished by Aurungzebe, who showed his zeal for Islam by building a mosque upon its site. Adjoining this division, and on the south-east of it, is one more recent, said to have been built principally by Saadat Ali, the Nawaub Vizier, who ruled in Oude from 1798 to 1814.

"The city is meanly built, the houses having generally mud walls, with roofs of straw; and many are no better than booths of mats and bamboos, thatched with palm-branches or leaves. The number of brickbuilt houses is small. With few exceptions, the streets, which are generally sunk ten or twelve feet below the level of the shops on each side, are crooked and narrow."

At the time this was written, Lucknow was ruled by a King of Oude, but the description given of the place as it was then, by no means applies to the present Station. I had prepared myself for a modernized impression; and certainly found my expectations more than agreeably realized.

When I sallied out in the morning, in what are called the civil lines, some mile and a half from the city proper, I was struck as much by

the marked absence of those usual accompaniments of a native city—dirt and confusion—as by the extreme purity and freshness of the atmosphere in comparison with that at Cawnpore and Allahabad. To this purity of atmosphere doubtless may be ascribable the remarkable preservation of the gilding on the many domes, minarets, and pinnacles everywhere surrounding you.

The first appearance of the place strikes one as fairy-like and most agreeable; but when the novelty wears off, you begin to discover a good deal of toy ornament about the many gaily decorated and painted buildings. Nevertheless, the extreme cleanliness of the Station, its broad and splendidly kept roads, green and neatly fenced maidans, and the many shady and beautiful trees around, with a general aspect of thorough control, supervision, and regularity—all these leave a most gratified impression on the mind; an impression certainly not eradicated in favour of any other Eastern city I have ever seen.

I was somewhat struck also with the very respectful demeanour of all classes of the natives, having till then understood that since the Mutiny they had become more upstart and insolent; and certainly having seen no evidence till then to the contrary.* Mentioning the circumstance to Major Chamberlain, the then worthy and energetic city magistrate, he told me that such insolence *had* been common enough shortly after the Mutiny, but that the evil had been remedied by promptly punishing all cases brought to notice, and that of late the public had had no reason to complain.

Such bazaars and native shops as are situated in the European portion of the city, are kept in a state of cleanliness and order quite marvellous to behold. There exists in Lucknow a municipal

* A native of Lucknow never addresses you without the prefix of *Ghurrib Purwur* (Protector of the Poor); and although in Bengal the titles of *Huzoor* and *Khodawund* (your Honour—your Lordship) are common enough, there lacks in the Lower Provinces that necessary attendant respect and fear without which the mere formal *utterance* is worthless indeed. Mr. Gubbins significantly relates the following in his account of the siege of Lucknow :—" It was amusing to notice the change in the demeanour of our native attendants towards us, as soon as they were assured that the garrison had really been relieved. . . . As the siege progressed, however, all conventionalities had been laid aside. *Sulams* were rarely seen; the posture of supplication never. Nothing more respectful than *ap* was heard, and *toom* (or "you") was not unfrequently substituted. This morning, therefore, I was not a little surprised at finding a row of domestics drawn up to receive me with the long-neglected *sulam.* It told me, as plain as words could have done, that the relative position of master and man, which had been so long interrupted, had again been restored."

commission apparently of some practical utility. This body receives the rents from the different confiscated buildings* now let out as shops, merchants' offices, and dwelling-houses, and expends the net income thus realized in improving and beautifying the city. There still remains much to be done, the portions near the river before referred to as having been cleared away, having left acres of building rubbish and broken ground which yet have to be levelled; but the vast reforms which have taken place since the Mutiny already indicate that it will not be many years before Lucknow can truly boast of being the model city of the East.

Lucknow has the credit, and apparently justly, of having been the original source from whence the Rebellion of '57 sprang. At the time Oude was annexed, no great significance seems to have been attached to the probability of its becoming the focus of intrigue, and the head-quarters of so great a rebellion as that which shook to its foundations our dominion in the East in 1857. Lord Dalhousie, writing in 1856, says: "The government of the province

* Some of the places now occupied as shops have been formerly *tombs*.

was assumed on the 7th of this month [February, 1856]. Up to the present time no resistance has been attempted—no disturbance of the public peace has occurred. The troops of the king are contentedly taking service in our pay; and thus far at least no zemindar or chief has refused submission to our authority. A complete civil administration had been prepared, and the military force which it was intended to retain had been fully organized, before negotiations were opened with the King. Officers had been named to every appointment. The best men that could be found available were selected from the civil and military services for the new offices in Oude, and the Government has every reason to anticipate that they will achieve an equal degree of success as those to whom similar tasks have previously been committed."*

How far these anticipations were realized is now patent to all. But there were not wanting those who at the time predicted the great danger which must inevitably result from the false sense of security into which the Government of India permitted itself to be lulled.

Lucknow, as the scene of the most remark-

* Minute of the Marquis of Dalhousie, 1856.

able siege on record, naturally possesses, apart from the intrinsic merit of its many noteworthy structures, a special interest; and it would hardly be fitting to record a mere description of its buildings, without adding information regarding the special incidents of which they were the scene during the terrible period of the Mutiny of 1857. Such a record must greatly add to the pleasure and information of any visiting these places, or seeking a knowledge on the subject. I have therefore been at some trouble to gather from friends on the spot, and from other reliable sources, all the pertinent facts in each case.

Lucknow can boast of several hospitals and asylums for the relief of the sick and the poor; principal amongst which may be named the Lunatic Asylum, and the *Khyrath Khana*, or the King's Charitable Refuge for Indigent Poor, supported from the interest of funds left in trust to the British Government by Nusseer-ood-deen Hyder. An infinity of good is unostentatiously effected by this charity, numbers being fed, clothed, and lodged. Then there is the King's Hospital, supported also by funds vested by Nusseer-ood-deen Hyder, to be used in perpetuity in affording gratuitous medicinal advice to all classes of natives; and the Eunanie Hospital, on the Greek system of treatment, known also as the Platonian system. Subsequent to the Mutiny, also, a Lock Hospital was instituted, and is well supported by voluntary contributions.

The south-eastern part of the city is skirted by the military cantonments, a series of well-built barracks in echelon, stretching from Dilkooshah to Alumbagh. These are capable of accommodating two line regiments, a cavalry regiment, besides several batteries of artillery; and the most elevated and open space around Lucknow appears to have been chosen for their site. The cantonments also contain a commodious if not a very handsome church, and a soldiers' institute, which is used as a theatre, lecture-room, &c.

Of course, the prominent features of interest in and about Lucknow are its public buildings, more especially those which played a part in the terrible period of the siege; and few there are which did not share more or less prominently in the stirring events of that notable time. Immediately subsequent to the Mutiny the several accounts of the siege of Lucknow which were then published, referred to these now celebrated structures; but only as they then appeared, and in immediate reference to their connection with the siege. Since then a wonderful change has been wrought in the city, and it is hardly recognizable as the Lucknow of 1857. Many of the edifices then in ruins from the hail of shot and shell have been repaired, altered, or pulled down; and so extensive have been the changes in one way and another, that a description of the city and the specialities of Lucknow as they now exist, from a traveller's point of view, is likely to be found novel and interesting.

Let us commence, then, from the furthermost building in the south-east quarter of the town, situate in a large park-like plain, and called—

THE DILKOOSHAH, OR HEART'S DELIGHT. This is an imposing square edifice with flanking towers and gilt dome. It was built by Saadut Ali Khan, as a country residence for himself and the ladies of his harem, and the jungle being cleared, a spacious park was laid out, which he stocked with game. The park is still there, almost denuded of wood, which has been used for fuel; and the game has also disappeared. At the entrance used by the ladies of the harem is a grand flight of steps leading up to a noble portico as high as the building. The Dilkooshah was prominent in the Mutiny of 1857 as forming the head-quarters of Sir Colin Campbell's force on the final attack and taking of Lucknow. It was also occupied after a smart skirmish by Sir Colin on his first advance to the relief of the Residency; and the relieved garrison lodged here on their way to Calcutta, in November, 1857.

The building itself is remarkably plain and unostentatious, but the rooms are spacious and apparently very comfortable. The view from the terrace over the park is extremely fine; and the residence was doubtless a most agreeable one, away from the heat and glare of the city. Mr. Russell, the *Times*' correspondent, graphically describes many a "warm reception" from the rebels who then occupied the Martinière, received by all who "showed" above the parapet of the roof; to which place, as affording a capital look-out, Sir Colin and his staff frequently resorted. Sir Colin, however, soon captured the position, and thus cleared away an important obstruction on his road to the Residency. Near to this building will run the new railway which is to connect Fyzabad, Lucknow, and Cawnpore. Not far distant from the Dilkooshah is—

THE LA MARTINIÈRE, or Constantia—a whimsical pile of buildings of every species of architecture, adorned with extravagant figures of animals and gods, in most fantastic array, with gaping mouths and shaking heads; while at the gateway or entrance there are two large flanking lions, so contrived that on gala days a lamp could be inserted into the hollows of their heads, lighting up the eyes and mouth. There are also several allegorical statues representing the seasons. These decorations had rather rough usage at the time of the Mutiny, and are now much defaced. The edifice is built tier upon tier, with four towers to the second tier, and semicircular wings to the lower, forming the front or approach. The top of the building is surmounted by a double crescent or hollow dome.

Constantia was erected by an eccentric French adventurer, who arrived in India a private soldier in Count Lally's famous division, which tried so hard to turn us out of Southern India. La Martine held local rank ultimately in the East-India Company's service, and died, possessed of enormous wealth, a major-general in the service of Asf-o-Dowlah. He seems to have been a kind of Jack-of-all-trades, and wondrously successful in his speculations: one of these was Constantia, designed for sale to the Nawab, who had offered, report says, to give the general a million of money for it when completed. Claude Martine, however, died before this event took place, and to prevent the property being seized by his not over-scrupulous master, ordered his body to be buried in it, which was done, and the buildings therefore respected.* It is stated that General Martine left £500,000 sterling to endow schools at Lucknow, Calcutta, and Lyons. The one under notice contains from 160 to 180 boys, who are provided with a substantial and useful education free of expense. If the school at Lyons is as well managed as those at Lucknow and Calcutta, the legacy of the general was wisely made, and has been faithfully administered.

The exterior of the building is imposing, but bizarre in effect and entirely wanting in harmony, from the eccentricities referred to. The interior is more artistic, but the space is much frittered away in long corridors and passages, so that the accommodation is quite disproportionate to the vast extent of ground the building covers. The ceilings of many of the rooms are very beautifully panelled in floral stucco relief and colour, and the walls of the principal

* A Mussulman will always respect a tomb. At the time of the Mutiny, however, the sepoys (Hindoos, I presume) broke open the vault containing the general's remains, in the hope of finding treasure.

chambers must have been, when in perfect preservation, strikingly beautiful; now, the decorations are considerably impaired. The principal of the College ascribed the injuries then observable to the mutineers; but expressed a belief that the cost of restoration would be too great to render it likely that the committee of management would sanction the undertaking. Facing the building is a lofty purposeless kind of column, something after the style of Nelson's Monument, standing in a sheet of water, but having no interior staircase or means of ascent. At the time of my visit this piece of water was being considerably enlarged to permit the drainage into it of the surrounding low land, the swampy nature of which it was believed caused ophthalmia to prevail, and had, the few previous seasons, seriously affected the health of the inmates of the school. From the top of the Martinière a superb view is obtained of the surrounding country, which from this elevation presents the appearance of being thickly wooded and richly cultivated.

The pupils of the Martinière did good service in the Residency during the siege, some in attending the hospitals, preparing the ammunition, and provisioning the inmates;

whilst others actively assisted in the defence of the place.

Leaving the Martinière, it is an easy drive to—

THE SECUNDER BAGH—built and laid out by Wajid Ali, for his wife the Secunder Mehal. It is a garden of 120 yards square, surrounded by a high wall of solid masonry. This wall had been loopholed by the rebels during the final relief of Lucknow; and from behind their screen the 2,000 defenders of the place kept up a fearful hailstorm of bullets on the 93rd Highlanders and 53rd Foot, who assaulted and took the place, and massacred the sepoys, it is said, to a man.*

Near to the Secunder Bagh is—

THE SHAH NUJEEF, where the troops in Sir Colin Campbell's advance to the relief of the Residency received a severe check. It is a tomb of Ghazee-ood-deen Hydur, the first King of Oude. It is easily distinguished by its flat white dome. In it are seen a series of pictures of the different Kings of Oude and favourites of the harem. An authority says, with reference to this place: "It derives its name from Nujuf, the hill on which the tomb of Ali, the son-in-law of Mahommed, is built, of

* The slain were found to be all sepoys of different mutineer regiments.

which tomb this building is said to be a copy. A fund was left by Ghazee-ood-deen to keep the place in repair, and to maintain an establishment of priests."

The following is the thrilling account of the storming of this place, as given by Mr. Gubbins:—"Behind a parapet, raised on the massive terrace of this tomb, the enemy were clustered, and poured a frightful fire on a company of the 90th, which got up within fifteen yards of the main building. They could discover, however, no entrance; and both subalterns who commanded it having been wounded, the men fell back behind some neighbouring huts. * * * The guns were now allowed to batter the place for two hours; after which Brigadier Hope was ordered to take it with the 93rd Highlanders. Finding that no breach had been effected, Brigadier Hope was obliged to send for a heavy gun, which was brought up by Captain Peel, of the *Shannon*, and was dragged by the sailors and men of the 93rd, under a fearful fire of musketry, close up to the wall of the Shah Nujeef. Here, with the muzzle almost touching the building, the 24-pounder was worked. The dust and smoke were so great that it was almost impossible to see what was the effect of this cannonade, unexampled except in naval warfare. A breach was made in the outer wall, but there was yet an inner wall, which seemed to present a serious obstacle, and the enemy from the elevated terrace still maintained a fire of musketry, which could not be effectually kept down by the rifles of the 93rd. There was a tree standing at the corner of the Shah Nujeef, close to the building, and at this juncture Captain Peel offered the Victoria Cross to any of his men who would climb it. Three men immediately ascended the tree up to the the level of the terrace, and from this position fired on the enemy. * * * By this time, however, the enemy, alarmed by the progress of the attack, began to desert the place. Their fire slackened: the Highlanders rushed in at the breach, and the Shah Nujeef was taken."

Between the Secunder Bagh and the Shah Nujeef lie the extensive gardens of the Agri-Horticultural Society of Oudh, bounded on the north by the Goomtee.

A *détour* to the left now brings you to Wingfield Park, a charmingly green and shady enclosure. The park is elegantly laid out, and richly studded with magnificent forest and other trees; the grounds affording a delightful drive and place of recreation for the residents of Lucknow. Leaving the park and passing the civil church, which is an elegant little structure, containing a very handsome stained glass window, you come upon the residence of the Chief Commissioner, or, as it was known before the Mutiny, Banks's Bungalow, from Major Banks, Commissioner of Lucknow.

It was in this building that the gallant Hodson, who received his death-wound in the attack on the Begum's Kothee, breathed his last. His men, however, exacted a terrible vengeance: for of all the defenders of the place not one escaped alive, and the clothes of the Sepoys taking fire, dead and wounded were involved in this fell holocaust.

Near thereto you will pass the ice-fields, where the "cooling agent" is manufactured during the cold season, and stored away in pits for use during the hot weather. Vast numbers of very shallow earthen pans are seen ranged in the open plain, which at sundown are regularly filled with water. Although up-country the thermometer is, even in winter, hardly ever below 65° in the daytime, the nights and early mornings are very cold and frosty—sufficiently so to deposit a thin covering of ice on water exposed in the open air. This is duly taken advantage of for "thirsty souls" living in "the

Station." During the night, a thin coating of ice is formed in the earthen pans, and before sunrise this is skimmed off, and stored in underground cellars for future use. In these days of progress, when ice can be made by steam, the old-fashioned, tedious, and expensive process of open-air ice manufacture will doubtless soon be a thing of the past in the larger Stations of Upper India; and we shall thus no more hear of that much dreaded event in an up-country station, caused by a more than ordinarily "warm" winter—"the failure of the ice-crop." Two large ice-machines have, I hear, been erected in the Station since I left.

Returning through the wide, clean, and extensive thoroughfare Huzrut Gunge, we pass the wholesome-looking market-place, and several large Mahomedan buildings with imposing painted gateways, one of which we will enter. It is the resting-place of Amjad Ali Shah, the father of the ex-King of Oudh. It consists of a large double square enclosing a considerable area; but the interior is in a very neglected state. A little below is the Begum's Kotee, now used as a post-office, which was the first line of defence taken by Outram's troops when making their way towards the

Kaiser Bagh. A breach was formed through the walls parallel with the Imambarra, and the troops thus enabled to advance free of the enemy's fire, which had been arranged to command only the road.

At the back of Amjad Ali's tomb, removed from the Huzrut Gunj Road, in an immense irregular pile called the Zuhoor Buksh, is a very extensive native printing-office, where missionary works, school books, &c., are printed in the vernacular, and where some one or two hundred men may be seen busily engaged in practising Guttenberg's mighty art in the most stolid manner possible, troubling themselves but little as to the results which are likely to flow from so wide-spread a diffusion of knowledge amongst an uneducated people. The seed, it is true, falls on hard ground, but some, nevertheless, takes root, and ultimate good cannot but accrue. Lucknow boasts its vernacular paper printed at this press. It is very extensively circulated, and eagerly read; but, unfortunately, the native Press does not, as a rule, set about its teachings or discussions in the way necessary to insure respect and attention.

Moving on in an easterly direction you next come to—

The Kaiser Bagh, which was erected by

the ex-King of Oudh, in 1850, at a cost, it is stated, of 80 lacs of rupees. Its shape is that of a series of quadrangles, approached through massive painted gateways, adorned with the regal emblem, "two fish embowed, and respecting each other," as the heralds have it. Incongruous as is the architecture of the place, and erratic as is the plan of its courts, gardens, pavilions, and avenues, it must have presented, in the days of its founder, a truly brilliant spectacle, surrounded with all the gaudy and striking appurtenances of an Eastern court, which knew no bounds to its extravagance.

The following is a very correct circumstantial account of the place, which I extract from a brief Lucknow Guide :—

"The Kaiser Bagh, the great work of the ex-King's reign, was commenced in 1848, and finished in 1850, A.D., at a cost (Wajid Ali's), including furniture and decorations, of eighty lacs. Kaiser is the same word as Cæsar, a title adopted by the kings of Oudh, and used by them on the royal seal to describe this palace. It will be best to suppose the visitor to enter at the north-east gateway, which faces the open space in front of the Tarawallie Kothie. Through this gate, and through a small gateway on the right hand, which is now closed up, the captives were conducted to their prison. We, however, pass up the open court in front of the gate called the Jillokhana, or place where the royal processions used to form and prepared to start from ; and turning to the right, through a gateway covered by a screen, we cross the Cheenie Bagh (so called from the large China vessels with which it was decorated), and going under a gate flanked by green mermaids, we come to the Huzrut Bagh. On the right hand we have the Chandiewallie Baradurrie, which used to be paved with silver, and the Kas Kukam and Badshah Munzil, which used to be the special residence of the king. His vizier, Nawab Ali Nukie Khan, used to reside above the mermaid gateway we have just passed under, in order that he might be close to the king, and obtain instant information of all he was doing. On the left we have the large confused pile of buildings called the Choulukie, built by Azeemoolah Khan, the royal barber, and sold by him to the king for 4 lacs. It formed the residence of the chief muhuls and of the queen. The rebel Begum held her court here, and it was in one of the stables near this that our captives were kept for weeks. Proceeding along the road-way, we pass close by a tree paved round the roots with marble, under which Wajid Ali used to sit in the days when the great fair was held, dressed in the yellow clothes of a Fakeer. Moving onwards, we pass under the great Lukhee-gate (so called from having cost a lac in building), and come into the magnificent open square of the Kaiser Bagh proper, the buildings round which were occupied chiefly by ladies of the Harem. In the month of August, a great fair used to be held here, to which the whole town was admitted. Proceeding past the Stone Baradurrie, fitted up as a theatre (but at present the assembly-rooms of the British Indian Association), and under the western Lukhee-gate, which corresponds to the eastern one just described, we have on our left the building known as the Kaiser Pusond, surmounted by a gilt semicircle and hemisphere. It was built by Roshun-o-Dowla, the vizier of Nuseer-od-deen Hyder, confiscated by Wajid Ali Shah, and given by him as a residence to a favourite muhul, Masook-ul-Sultan (it is now used for public offices). On the right is another Jillokhana, corresponding to the eastern one, by which we entered the palace; and turning down it, we find ourselves outside the Kaiser Bagh, and opposite the Sher Durwaza, or Neill gateway, under which General Neill was killed by a discharge of grape-shot from a gun posted at the gate of the Kaiser Bagh, which we have just left. [Marshman, in his Memoirs of Havelock, says, he was shot from an upper room.]

Between the great quadrangle of the Kaiser Bagh and the Cheenie Bazaar stand the two tombs of Sadut Ali Khan (called after his death, by a sort of apotheosis, Jinnut Aramgah, or the one whose soul is in Paradise) and of his wife Murshid Zadie. Both these tombs were built after their death by their son Ghazee-ood-deen Hyder, who thereby displayed a very uncommon amount of filial affection. The spot on which the Sadut Ali's tomb now stands was formerly occupied by a house in which Ghazee-ood-deen Hyder lived during his father's reign, and it is reported that, when he came to the throne and occupied Sadut Ali's palace, fully appreciating the change in their respective situations, he remarked that, as he had now taken his father's house, it was but fair that he should give up his own to his father. Accordingly, he gave orders to destroy his former abode, and raise on the site a tomb to Sadut Ali Khan.

Almost facing the Kaiser Bagh, on the other side of the road and separated by an enclosed green plot neatly railed in, is—

THE TARAWALLEE KOTIE, formerly the Observatory, and now the Bank of Bengal. The enclosed space in front is memorable as the spot where, during the mutiny, the massacre of the English captives sent in by the Dhowzear

Rajah and the Mithowlie Rajah took place, after they had suffered a dreadful series of indignities and hardships. The memorial erected on the spot gives the names of most of the sufferers. It is satisfactory to know, however, that the prime instigators and abettors of these deeds, Rajah Joylal Singh, Bundeh and Futteh Ali, were ultimately discovered and hung in sight of the very spot they had made infamous by their sanguinary cruelty.

You now get a very pleasing view of the river Goomtee, which is crossed here by a bridge of boats, and lower down by an iron and stone bridge.* The former is a not inelegant structure, commenced in the time of Nusser-ood-deen, but not completed until the reign of Mahomed Ali Shah (about 1840). The stone bridge is a clumsy edifice, built by Asf-o-Dowla, about 1780, A.D.

It was along the stone bridge that the rebels escaped on the capture of Lucknow. Our troops were insufficient in number to occupy both this and the iron bridge, at which latter, however, we had guns posted, playing on the former, and these did terrible execution amongst the flying rebels.

* A second iron bridge has just been commenced at this spot.

The Goomtee near the bridge of boats is extremely picturesque, and much resembles in size the Thames at Richmond. In the rains, however, the water rises considerably, and resembles a swollen torrent. The illustration annexed represents it in its more placid mood. In front are seen the palaces of the Chuttur Munzil and the Furhud Bux; and to the extreme right, in the background, are the ruins of the Residency, with the now half-shattered tower in which Sir Henry Lawrence received his death wound. Across the bridge of boats, and about a quarter of a mile down the road, are the remains of one of the King's gardens—

THE BADSHAH BAGH. The mutineers held this place during the siege, and terribly annoyed the Residency garrison by a constant cannonade. The shell which killed Sir Henry Lawrence was fired from this position. The place is now a desolate ruin, but it is worth a visit for the purpose of seeing the cultivation of the silkworm, there carried on by Dr. Bonavia. On racks round the rooms (which bear the evidence of former state and grandeur, some of the marble with which the walls of the centre hall was lined still remaining) are ranged trays containing thousands upon thousands of silkworms in every stage of

LUCKNOW—BRIDGE OF BOATS

growth, the yield of silk from which must be something very considerable.

Dr. Bonavia has kindly furnished me with the following account of the treatment of the silkworm in his "Nursery":—"Experiments were commenced with silkworms of various kinds in the beginning of 1863. At first it was difficult to keep the Bengal varieties alive throughout the year. The winter in Lucknow was too cold for them, and the summer too hot, but by some trouble they are now kept alive throughout the twelve months, so that they can be rapidly multiplied at the seasons in which they thrive best, that is, during the whole of the rains and at the end of the winter months. They are reared exactly in the Bengal way, the natives of Lucknow having been taught by Bengalees. The silk is roughly reeled off the cocoons, after the Bengal method. There being no market, for the finer kinds of silk, they are not produced. All that has been done in Lucknow yet, has been on an experimental scale, as it is impossible to say whether silkworm-rearing in Oudh will pay commercially.

"Various experiments with silkworms are being made in other parts of Oudh, and eggs have been furnished from time to time from the Lucknow Conservatory. Experiments have been also made with the Cashmere silkworm and the Bengal animal. The former does not thrive very well, but the latter has so far succeeded well, although there is some difficulty in procuring mulberry leaves in large quantities at the only time the Bengal animal hatches, viz., winter."

The gardens contain the remains of an extensive series of aqueducts and ornamental waterworks of curious design, which, when in order, must have imparted a delightful aspect of coolness to the spot. There is no other place of interest on this side of the river, with the exception of the unfinished tomb of the debauched Nusseer-ood-deen Hyder, which is hardly worth a visit. The two "gaswork-chimney"-looking minarets can be seen from the Residency across the Goomtee, and a nearer inspection is not at all desirable.

Returning hence, and proceeding along the river bank, we come to the two prominent buildings on the left, seen in the preceding illustration — the Chuttur Munzil and the Furhud Bux. The former is so named from the gilt umbrellas with which it is adorned, or, as some say, from its being four-storied, and was built by Nusseer-ood-deen as a residence for the ladies of his harem. The Furhud Bux was occupied by the King himself as his city palace, and is frequently referred to and fully described by Knighton, in his *Private Life of an Eastern King.*

Before the advance of Havelock, these buildings were occupied also by the enemy, who kept up from thence a destructive fusillade on the Bailey Guard defences. But on the first relief of the garrison, the palaces were stormed and included in the new and extended line of defence arranged by General Outram. The buildings have a light and graceful appearance, and command a fine prospect. They are now used as a club-house, a public library, and for Government offices. One of this pile, a large red-looking structure, called the Lal Baradurie, has been fitted up as a museum. It is only, however, in its infancy at present.

It was by the road just along the line of the Furhud Bux, Chuttur Munzil, Secunder Bagh, Martinière, and Dilkooshah, that the rescued Lucknow garrison passed *en route* to the Alumbagh; screens having been erected during the night to cover and conceal the most exposed portions of the road from the enemy's observation. The retirement of the garrison without any casualty, along a route covered in many places by the enemy's fire, speaks much for the cautious skill of Sir Colin, who personally directed and supervised the evacuation.

We now come to the most historically interesting of all the sights of Lucknow—

THE WORLD-RENOWNED RESIDENCY.—This is approached through the well-remembered "Bailey Guard" Gate,* which stands now in its solemn ruin, a monument alike of the bravery and devotion of that handful of heroes who held it for five months successfully against overwhelming numbers, and of the self-denying heroism of the women and children who died uncomplainingly in its cellars. Little now remains of the buildings which, in 1857, formed the Residency and its defences. The position of the beleagured garrison must have been very much more extended than is generally supposed. The Residency building itself only afforded accommodation to about one-fifth of the besieged. Many other large buildings, including the residences of the different Com-

* The origin of this name is thus stated: at first no military guard was attached to the officer acting for the British Government as Resident of Lucknow; but when Colonel Bailey held this office, a guard of honour was appointed, and a house built for it by Saadut Ali close to the gate of the Residency enclosure, which thus obtained its world-famous name of the Bailey Guard gate.

missioners, the post-office, and the jail, were within what are rather mis-named the entrenchments. Thus "the Residency" must have been quite a quarter of a mile in diameter in places.

Such of the walls and rooms as are standing bear the impress everywhere of shot and shell, constant streams of which compelled the removal of the ladies and children to the Tyekhanah or underground apartments. So exposed, indeed, was the position on all sides held by the defenders, that it was only necessary for one of the garrison to be seen, to ensure a shower of bullets from the adjoining houses. Major Banks, upon whom the chief control devolved on the death of Sir Henry Lawrence, was killed thus while incautiously raising his body above the parapet of an outhouse to view the enemy.

A crowd of buildings of all kinds surrounded the Residency position, and on one occasion the enemy were within *twelve feet* of the houses in the Residency compound. One who had served in the garrison told me that, on a mine being sprung, the outer wall of one of the houses occupied by the garrison fell down, and the defenders found themselves within jumping distance of the sepoys in an adjoining house, who, however, lacked the courage to rush forward: had they done so, this line of defence must have been taken. Protected even as were the underground apartments, on one occasion a shell found its way through the wall, killing and maiming the defenceless inhabitants.

Sir Henry Lawrence, who occupied a room on the first story of the north-east of the building, a position greatly exposed to the enemy's fire, had, it appears, been previously entreated to remove to some safer quarters, but had refused; notwithstanding, also, that on the 1st of July a shell had entered the room and burst in it. On the following day, the natives having by this time made sure their aim, another shell entered, but with more deadly results, shattering Sir Henry Lawrence's leg, and causing his lamented death on the fourth of the same month.

At the time of my visit the foundation was preparing for a memorial monument adjoining, which has probably by this time been completed, and it is hoped that the Government will not stop here, but enclose the ruins themselves, sufficiently restoring them to prevent total destruction, and enclosing and guarding them as a memorial and warning of the terrible past.

A little in advance of the Residency, to the west and north-west of the building, where Lawrence was killed, is the church-yard, where many a gallant soldier and helpless victim lie sleeping. The chapel attached was destroyed during the mutiny, but the grave-yard has been restored, and is now kept in elegant order. Here is the tomb of Sir Henry Lawrence, with the simple inscription — "*Here lies Henry Lawrence, who tried to do his duty.*" Near to this spot is the tomb of the gallant Neill, and around are the graves also of many of his brave compatriots. The inscriptions on the tombs are of a pure and simple character, and those of the little children, who died of wounds or of privation during the siege, are, as may be imagined, most touching. What the sufferings of these poor creatures must have been, confined in the vaults of the Residency in this, the hottest, season of the year, deprived of suitable food and exposed to all the horrors of so barbarous a siege, it is terrible to contemplate; and the marvel is, not that so many died, but that any at all survived. And the tear starts unbidden to the eye at the recollection of those crowded cells, where wailing infants and suffering women with brave endurance passed those five weary months of the siege, waiting for that release which, to but too many, led only to the neighbouring church-yard. For long you remain near this spot, and gaze at the Residency with feelings of pride, mingled with grief and sorrow. May many a century pass before another such occurrence darkens the land, and may our rulers so act, and be so prepared with the strong arm, that the bare thought of rebellion may, if it be possible, die out from the hearts of the treacherous sons of the soil.

A short distance in advance of the Residency stands—

THE MUCHEE BHOWAN FORT.—This was formerly the stronghold of the Seikhs in years long gone by, and is situated on the main road leading from the Residency towards the Hoseynabad. At the wish of Sir Henry Lawrence, an attempt was made to fortify and provision it on the first serious indication of disturbances, in 1857. It was at this time closely surrounded by houses, and considered by the engineers of the time (as it ultimately proved to be) quite untenable. It was abandoned, in great part blown up, and the guns spiked, on the night of the 30th of June, 1857; the garrison effecting this, and their junction with the residency troops, without the loss of a single man. It is believed that had the attempt to hold both the

Muchee Bhowan and Residency been persevered in, both must have fallen, from the numerical weakness of the defensive force. The fort has since been repaired, enlarged, and altered, and all surrounding houses cleared away from its vicinity; but it is not even now much relied on as capable of any prolonged defence. A strong military position is in course of construction at Char-Bagh, the southern entrance to the city, which will enclose the railway station, the arsenal, and enough accommodation for the European residents in case of an emeute.

We now arrive at the great architectural gem of Lucknow. Entering through a pair of lofty imposing double gates, and passing from an inner court under a large gateway on the left, you enter the enclosure of—

The Great Imambarra.—This truly magnificent hall, said to be the largest in the world, stands on an elevated terrace approached more immediately from two vast square courts, richly laid with tesselated pavements, the innermost court being elevated considerably above the other, adding thus to the effect of the building as viewed from below. It is described as "The crowning work of Nawab Asf-o-dowla's reign. He is said to have spent incredible sums on it, and the native report, always prone to exaggerate, puts the cost at a million sterling. The architects were invited to submit their plans to a competition, Asf-o-dowla only stipulating that the building should be no copy of any other work, and that it should surpass anything of the kind ever built in beauty and magnificence. Kyfeeut-ool-lah was the name of the successful competitor, and it would be hard to say that its conception, as it stands before us in the present day, falls at all short of the large and liberal stipulations of the monarch. The building is as solid as it is graceful, built from very deep foundations, and no wood-work is used throughout."

The Great or Royal Imambarra is now used as an arsenal, and, fitted with the stern implements of war, it presents a striking contrast to what it must have done when in the time of its splendour. The great hall is 162 feet long by 53 ft. 6 in. wide, and lofty in proportion, with carved and highly ornamented roof. On the two sides are verandahs, respectively 26 ft. 6 in. by 27 ft. 3 in.; and at each end is a fine octagonal apartment, 53 ft. in diameter, the whole interior dimensions being thus 263 ft. by 145. At the death of its founder he was interred here, but during his lifetime it was probably used as the grand celebration place for the Mohurrum;

since Knighton, in his *Private Life of an Eastern King*, observes that an Imambarra is a building raised by the sect of Moslems called Sheeahs, for the celebration of the Mohurrum; and he describes in another chapter the Mohurrum as kept in the time of Nusseer-o-deen in, as I take it, this very building:—"The Imambarra on this day was fitted up, of course, with extraordinary splendour, and when the preparations were complete, the public were admitted to gaze upon the glittering, although somewhat *bizarre*, scene. They crowded the vast hall in thousands; some admiring the strangely-varied collection of chandeliers, one of which alone, as I well remember, contained more than a hundred wax-lights."

On the capture of the Imambarra by Sir Colin Campbell, at the taking of Lucknow, these chandeliers, mirrors, and the like, were ruthlessly destroyed by our infuriated troops; and Mr. Russell describes the marble floor as having been three inches thick with the débris of the valuable decorations it contained. To the right of the Imambarra stands a copy of the Delhi Jumma Musjid, having two lofty four-storied minars or towers, an ascent to the upper galleries of which is rewarded by a truly superb view of the city and surrounding country.

The Great Imambarra stands near the Room-i-Durwâzâ or Constantinople Gate of Lucknow —a gate built, it is asserted, on the model of that which gave to the Court of the Sultan of Turkey the title of "The Sublime Porte." The gate is grand and elegant in style, and well harmonizes with the Imambarra itself. Much of the effect, however, which would otherwise be produced by the magnificent structures in Lucknow, is lost from very sameness. The architecture all partakes more or less of the same character, as do also the decorations of the buildings. The designs are pure Moresque in most cases, and the Palace of the Alhambra will give, in its various parts, a copy of almost all the styles of stone carving and decoration in Lucknow.

It is stated that both the Roumie Durwaza and the Great Imambarra were undertaken in a year of great famine, to provide the starving population with bread; but judging from the system of forced labour then prevailing, and from the capricious acts of the kings of those times, I should be inclined to attribute the origin of these works to a far more personal ambition.

The next notable building, and one closely adjoining the Great Imambarra, is—

The HOSEINABAD IMAMBARRA. It was erected by Mahomed Ali Shah, the successor of the "Eastern King" described by Knighton. This man, the uncle of Nusseer-o-deen, reigned only four years, and does not appear to have performed any other noteworthy act than the building of this place, and of a large tank adjoining. He commenced, however, close by, a Musjid, which was intended to surpass anything of the kind, as well as a seven-storied watch-tower. But his death interrupted both, and the unfinished remains are still as they were at that time. The Hoseinabad Imambarra is, in comparison with its grander neighbour, insignificant, but nevertheless of great beauty of execution and finish in detail. It stands in a large quadrangle, occupied in the centre by a marble reservoir of water, crossed by a fanciful iron bridge. On the water floats an ugly punt, with a very admirably executed model, made in England, of the Nawab's favourite charger. The quadrangle is, for its size, injudiciously crowded with buildings and contains a very poor model of the Taj at Agra. The Hall itself is filled with massive but old-fashioned mirrors and enormous upright chandeliers, standing ten feet high, and hung with all kinds of coloured glass globes. A great number of chandeliers also hang from the roof, and with the crystal and coloured globes and glass ornaments with which the place is filled, and the stained and painted windows, the effect when illuminated must be wondrously brilliant. The throne of the King, covered with beaten silver, and his Begum's divan of solid silver supports, velvet hangings, and silver ceiling-work, are also seen here.

In the open court, along the parapet of the fountains, up the pillars, across cornices, and on every conceivable inch of brickwork and plaster, are iron sconces for lamps, which, in the Mohurrum, are duly lighted. It must truly, at that time, be a sight worth seeing, and I only regretted I could not stay for it.

Tired almost with gazing at the gorgeous effect of the pure white marble and lofty ornamented roofs of these wonderful structures, we returned to our hotel, having made arrangements, through the kindness of Major Chamberlain, to see the native quarter of the town in the only way that it can properly be seen, viz., from the back of an elephant.

It takes, properly speaking, three days fully to explore the city of Lucknow. I had already spent two in viewing the various places of interest here described, and the third day I devoted to a visit to the Bazaars, to the Secunderabagh, Shah Nujeef, and to a charming country ride through a diverging road leading behind the town towards that point where the Alumbagh forms the apex of the junction of this road with the Grand Trunk Road from Cawnpore. It now only remained, therefore, to make this visit to the native city.

An elephant having been procured, we proceeded in the cool of the afternoon to the entrance of the chowk, or principal native bazaar of the town, here approached through a large archway; and mounting the howdah of the huge beast, which knelt at a word from the *mahout* to receive us, entered the narrow tortuous windings of the Lucknow native town. Great numbers of people were to be found outside the bazaar, carrying on a desultory trade in all kinds of edibles; but anything approaching the multitude that swarmed in the heart of the bazaar itself, I have never seen. The sagacious elephant passed unconcernedly along, his huge carcass threatening apparently every now and then to sweep away some block of buildings round which it seemed otherwise impracticable to proceed. In advance, shouting and clearing the way, ran the *hattiwan*, our advance guard; the crowds on foot making way with good grace as we swept loftily along,—our heads level with the second stories of the buildings on either side, the rickety overhanging verandahs of which were seen filled with lounging men, women, and children—smoking, sleeping, shaving, eating, doing anything and everything, in fact, but working. Such of the houses as were one-storied only had their flat roofs crowded with people of all ages and both sexes, occupied in the like task of doing nothing, the occupants being dressed in bright yellow, green, and red coloured cloths, spangled tissues, and pointed slippers, as the taste and means of the wearer permitted. Fronting a mosque built in the angle of the wall of a house, on the second story, knelt a score of clean-robed Mussulmen, their heads covered with the clean white cotton skull-cap, alternately (in most accurate unison) bending themselves flat to the ground, and rising with folded arms and downcast eyes, solemnly engaged in the task of performing their devotions, utterly unmindful of the Babel of noise around them.

In the tiny shops below—some straight, some crooked; some high, some low; some projecting boldly in advance of others which for no apparent reason seemed to have retired modestly into an almost hidden nook—men of every trade and calling were sitting enthroned among their wares, sitting as a native only *can* sit, with the calves of the leg doubled flat against the thigh, elbow on knees, smoking dirty hubblebubbles, which ever and anon they handed round;—but not, you would think, as a "calumet of peace," for each one seemed quarrelling vociferously with his neighbour, *pice* (money) being apparently the prevailing general topic.

Here was to be seen a young city "swell," the son of some native *burra saheb* (great man) in his gold-spangled skull-cap, and tight-fitting bright-spangled tissue surtout, with red or green trousers worn tight to the leg, his feet gaily clothed with tinsel-covered pointed shoes—preceded by a couple of fierce-looking six-feet outriders, their red turbans folded gracefully round the head, and the long fringed ends hanging picturesquely over their shoulders.

Then there appeared a curious kind of *araba*, or bullock-carriage, creaking lazily along, the sitting part of the vehicle sloping at a considerable angle downwards from the yoke, in most uncomfortable-looking fashion; the interior of the "carriage" being fitted gaily with scarlet cloth, and filled with a family of women and children, shrouded to the eyes, huddled knees to nose, all of a heap, while *pater familias* stalked proudly by the side, holding a five-feet high walking-cane. Above the vehicle hung a dome-shaped scarlet canopy, fringed with tassels, while the bells on the necks of the oxen jangled musically as they journeyed lazily on.

Next came a knot of gaily-clothed eager talkers, demonstrating some particular theory with all the energy of which their lungs were capable; and, in marked contrast, a file of almost nude coolies, carrying leviathan loads on their heads, and shouting as they jostled unceremoniously the noisy beggar, exposing his sores, yelling forth his woes, and soliciting alms.

Imagine this motley throng—all vociferating one against another, each as regardless of, and unconcerned at, the presence of any one else as if he were alone; and—having further imagined a combination of every known and unknown odour—you will have some idea of the bazaar, or chowk, of the city of Lucknow. Yet with all this reigned the most perfect order, and considerably more outward cleanliness than is observable in a Calcutta bazaar; and, although the roadway was but some ten feet wide, there seemed to be room for everybody. Contrast this with the state of things which existed in the reign of the few last kings of Lucknow, when the streets were thronged with armed retainers of the different men of rank of the city, between whom party conflicts were of almost daily occurrence. Even those pious folk who declaim against the British spoliation of Oude territory must admit that society, as well as the native, has at any rate gained by the transfer.

And that this was the normal state of Indian regal custom, and not attributable to any special circumstance, we have only to refer to history to determine. Even in our time, in the person of the last of the kings of Oude, what do we find? A debauched and prematurely-old man—the slave of his parasites; powerless now perhaps for political evil, but potent for such as flows from example; the receiver of a truly royal income, but inextricably burdened with debt.

Let us follow a little further the history of this representative of a once powerful dynasty, and see how he bears his altered state, and whether misfortune has brought with it wisdom and an altered life.

The visitor to Calcutta who approaches that city by its great water highway, the Hooghly River, will, after passing the long low lines of flat green land immediately above the famed Botanical Gardens, come suddenly upon a series of fantastically-painted villas — some grey, some yellow, some blue — standing in extensive garden enclosures, ornamented more by nature than by art. Tinselly-looking trellis screens are dotted about the river bank in front, as if to shut out from vulgar gaze the sacred interior, where dovecotes, kiosks, and summer-houses appear in plenty. A purposeless kind of outer verandah, some hundred yards long, of the suburban tea-garden order of architecture, is seen perched on the top of a newly-erected river wall, which might be considered, and was evidently intended, as an improvement on the slimy mud frontage it in part occupies; only, like the throne of the Moguls, it has an irreparable fissure in it, from top to bottom; and the verandah has in consequence received an awkward twist, foreboding a not remote descent into the dirty stream beneath. Nevertheless, it affords an apparently pleasant resting-place for innumerable white-robed and gaily-shawled gentlemen, who lounge on the benches above the reeking mud, as if they really enjoyed it. These dignitaries are part of the suite of the Ruler of the Universe and Light of the World—Wajid Ali Shah, ex-King of Oude, whose palace, surmounted by a gilt sun, stands a few yards off. Old residents of Calcutta remember well the time when that building was one of the most charming of European residences, boasting the loveliest of gardens, and with its sister villas delightfully situate along the river's bank, justifying the reputation which Calcutta enjoyed, as the city possessing the most beautiful approach of any in the world. Now, who that has not known the place of yore could believe what it once was. Long lines of stable-like buildings, occupied by the thousand and one menials of the ex-King, constitute the boundary on either side which of old was marked only by waving palms and giant flowering shrubs. The peaceful charm of the spot in years gone by, its quiet placid beauty and air of utter repose, are replaced by the harsh discordance of native tom-tom and drum; and the thousands who now live in and crowd about its outer approaches, revelling in all the filth, disorder, turmoil, and licence of a native Court, are a painful contrast to the rural and tranquil appearance of the Garden Reach of only a few years past.

It will be remembered that on the annexation of Oude by the Marquis Dalhousie, the then occupant of the musnud, Wajid Ali Shah, uncle of Nusseer-o-deen, was granted a pension of thirteen lacs of rupees (£130,000) a year, and permitted to fix his residence at Garden Reach, the extreme inhabited part of Calcutta proper. This situation possessed many advantages over others, for its object. It was in the outskirts of the town, had ample land accommodation, and was overlooked by the Fort, and in full view of the docks and shipping. Accordingly, a handsome and commodious residence, formerly occupied by Sir Laurence Peel, was appropriated and converted into an abode for his ex-Majesty. Gradually the villas on either side, and facing the grounds, were purchased; lofty walls and high mat fences in time took the place of fragrant and verdant hedgerows. Tatterdemalion sepoys mounted guard at the gates. Prime ministers, officers of state, and their myriad hangers-on, swooped like locusts upon the revenues of the unfortunate prince, and fastened themselves like horse-leeches upon and around him. Soon they, too, began to build fantastic structures. Bazaars sprung up in the outer walls of these; isolated, picturesque huts grew into dirty crowded villages with the rapidity of tropical growth. The imprisonment of the King during the period of the Mutiny stopped the ruin for a time, and all fell into neglect; till, on his release and full restoration to the large allowance granted him, Garden Reach became for miles suddenly transformed into the similitude of a Bear-garden, where riot, licentiousness, and extravagance, which can only end in utter bankruptcy, reigned unchecked. Such, indeed, it now is; and flagrant violation of the law is only prevented by the location of a police force in the heart of the place, which for all purposes of beauty and recreation, as of yore, is for ever destroyed.

From what is seen and known of this shadow of a native court, under all the restrictions which its immediate proximity to the seat of the Supreme Government imposes, some idea may be formed of what must have been the state of affairs in Lucknow, where the only limit was the will of the monarch, and its exercise the cupidity of those by whom he was surrounded.

CHAPTER VII.

AGRA.

Akberabad—Its former Splendour—An expensive Cab-fare—Indian Beggars—The "Traveller's Rest"—Bargaining—The Taj; How we treat a Tomb—The Taj as seen by Blue Lights—Soap-stone Carvings—The Fort—Futtehpore Sikree—Tomb of Akbar.

RETURNING to Cawnpore in time for the up night train, which can be managed by starting from Lucknow early in the morning, the rail takes you in about eight hours to Toondla Junction, from whence a branch line runs to Agra. As the train whirls you along towards the once famed city of Akberabad, it is impossible to help moralising on the wondrous changes which have occurred since the days when the Mussulman dynasty held sway over these rich and fertile countries. Here possibly, where now speeds the all-civilizing locomotive, the hordes of Timour the Tartar swept, devastating, over the plain; or from the city which bears his name, and which now appears to our view, the battalions of Akbar the Magnificent, in all the pomp and splendour of unbounded Eastern wealth, delighted the eye, as they struck terror into the heart, of the worshipping thousands who flocked from the city to greet the mighty emperor.

The city of Agra, the capital of the great Akbar, stands on the left bank of the Jumna, and in the days of its splendour the space from the river's bank to the fort is said to have been covered with palaces. Of these nought is now seen but ruins. Much of this is the result of natural decay. They are still picturesque in their fall. Others, however, are the *débris* of clearances effected since the Mutiny by our iconoclastic Government, and these, it need hardly be said, add little charm to the scene. Time, which has wrought such destruction as is now to be witnessed, will doubtless, in a few years, bring some more appropriate order out of the prevailing chaos, and Agra may thus become, as it needs, permanently improved in appearance—improved in a modern sense. From the impression I had formed and the accounts I had heard of this famous city, I was quite unprepared for the irregular and disorderly place I found it. The railway, however, lands you at the commencement of the native town, in as dusty and uninteresting a locality as you can well imagine, and your first approach to Agra thus in some degree prepares you for the ruin and disorder you afterwards see around.

The traveller will not, however, be too particular about these first impressions, for he knows that the true glories of Agra will yet delight his eye anon. Indeed, one is only too glad to be rid of the noisy train, to shake off some of the dust of travel, and to jump into the gharry at the station, ramshackle though it be. I confess to having been somewhat startled by Jehu's demand of 3rs. 12as.* (seven shillings and sixpence) for taking us into the town; but one gets used to these things in India. So, having rescued our traps from a dozen coolies, who were endeavouring to take possession of them on our behalf, into the vehicle we jumped. "*Bucksheesh, sahib, bucksheesh!*" shout a horde of little naked dusty imps. "*Allah illam*——" commences a poor bent crone, thrusting her shrivelled palm into the gharry for some pice; but as you espy a

* The twelve annas are to pay the Bridge of Boats' toll, there being a similar nuisance here in this respect to the one at Cawnpore; only with this difference, that the former is the more troublesome of the two.

train of beggars, halt, blind, and maimed, about to besiege you in like manner, you endeavour —but, alas! without avail—to bring together the two panels of the sliding-door, which, warped irrecoverably by the weather, refuse to move an inch. Observing your helplessness, the crowd of mendicants press towards you. "*Chellao! chellao!*—Go on! go on!"—This to the gharriwan. "*Acchha, sahib,*—All right, sir." Then why doesn't he move? It is Rosinante who objects. Until, by the aid of a couple of "vulgar little boys" at the wheels, the gharry begins to stir, and you are off; presently jolting most uncomfortably over the rickety plank bridge which forms the only means of approach to renowned Akberabad.

Having heard a hotel called the Traveller's Rest greatly extolled, we drove there. A fine-looking Mussulman, Hossein Khan, the proprietor, appeared, and welcomed us on alighting. What's in a name? Well, friend Hossein did the honours of his caravanserai amiably enough; but his idea of external comfort and ours did not precisely tally; and in the matter of the *cuisine*—Bah! why should a devout Mussulman so carefully gauge the palate of an infidel? It was too late, however, to turn back to *the* hotel of Agra—Beaumont's; so we placidly threw ourselves to rest,—tired, and not over-particular, on our charpoys, and dreamed of—mosquitoes.

The traveller to Agra has four places of special interest to visit, viz. Futtehpore Sikree, the Taj, the Fort, and Akbar's Tomb at Secundra. From the distance of the former, some twenty-four miles, and the necessity of arranging a day previously for a conveyance, it is found desirable to make this the last place of visit. The hotel-keeper will generally supply a dâk; but if not, you have a host of offers at your service at prices ranging from 25rs. to 40rs. the journey. And here a capital opportunity for a little bargaining is afforded. A native would feel utterly disconcerted if you gave him what he asked, for in that case he would never cease to regret that he had not asked you more. On the other hand, you enter into negotiations with him with the distinct knowledge that he is asking about double what he will take. Accordingly an animated conversation ensues, which ends in both being satisfied: the native is consoled that he has, after all, done you, while you flatter yourself that this time you *have* got a bargain.

These trifling but very essential preliminaries adjusted, and a gharry procured, the blinds of which were warranted to act, we proceeded, in the cool of the morning, to visit the world-renowned Taj, which is about a two miles' drive from Agra, on the left bank of the Jumna, upwards. The white dome of the building is visible from almost every point of the city, but as seen at a distance from the level plain, it does not appear to advantage. It is only when viewed from a height, or seen from within the garden of the Taj itself, and in full sight of its exquisite outline and proportions, that the descriptions one has heard and read of it become fully realized. As an old writer says: "It is like some bright and newly-discovered winged thing, all beauteous in a beauty peculiar to itself, and referable to no class or order on the roll of zoology, which the whole world flocks to gaze upon with silent delight, none presuming to designate the lovely stranger nor to conjecture a kindred for it with the winged thing of earth. Suffice it—Love was its author; Beauty its inspiration."

The enclosure of the Taj—a parallelogram of 1,860 feet by more than 1,000, is surrounded by arcades, and adorned by four noble gateways, the principal of which measures 110 feet by

140. It is built of red sandstone, elaborately carved, and inscribed with illuminated verses from the Koran. In these superb buildings—for such they may fairly claim to be—are rooms let out to travellers by the authorities; and a more charming way of spending a few days I can scarcely imagine. A residence here, for a short time, affords a most pleasurable opportunity of studying fully the inexhaustible beauties of the place, and breathing the fresh pure air of the surrounding gardens.

Although justification may thus be found for the diversion of these buildings to a use certainly never contemplated by their founder, it is very questionable how far the profanation of the grounds to the purposes of noisy pleasure and picnic parties is warrantable. The place is still the abode of the dead, and should, I think, receive at our hands a greater show of respect than we deem it necessary to display. What feelings our treatment of the place must arouse in the breast of the pious Mussulman, it is not difficult to imagine.

From the principal gateway, whence a fine centre view of the Taj is commanded, you descend by a few broad stone steps into a garden full of magnificent and sweet-scented shrubs, fruit, and other trees, the beds being

THE TA

richly adorned, also, with flowers of many brilliant hues. The pathways are of stone, and down the centre of the garden is a long reservoir with fountain-jets at intervals, the walks on either side being planted with lofty and thickly-clothed cypresses. The fountains were not playing at the time of our visit, but I understood they were in perfect order, and were used on high-days and holidays.

Proceeding to the end of the paved court, you ascend a few steps to a large tesselated marble platform, from which a flight of marble steps in the wall leads to a terrace of marble, 313 feet square (marble, thus, everywhere), upon which stands the beautiful pile itself, occupying a square of 186 feet, with the corners cut off, as seen in the drawing.

At the extreme corners of this dazzling platform are four lofty minarets. They are of exquisite proportions, and of the smallest possible circumference in proportion to their height, which is 133 feet. From the roof-centre springs the marble dome, expanding grandly, and rising to a height of 80 feet, tipped on its summit with a gilt crescent-pointed spire, 296 feet from the basement. This mighty dome is supported on the four corners of the roof-terrace by as many smaller domes, enhancing greatly the effect of the larger. I will not attempt further to describe in detail the building externally, but refer the reader to the annexed illustration for some conception of the beauty of outline and proportion, to the enchanting effect of which no pen or pencil, I believe, can do sufficient justice.

On either side of the Taj, on the ground beneath, is a red-sandstone building, also with lofty domes and handsome portals. These are termed the *jawabs*, or answers, and are supposed to have been erected to enhance, by force of contrast, the beauty of the main building itself. Being themselves of no mean pretensions in point of grandeur and beauty, they serve to show, at any rate, a more than regal disregard of cost in the desire to secure the greatest possible effect, which dictated the magnificent conception before us.

But it is time to enter the Taj itself. At the doors lie the slippers of the Faithful by dozens; but although it is not necessary for the traveller to follow the example, he will not fail to be impressed with the solemn and almost sacred feeling which the building, on its first entrance, inspires. Entering the dazzlingly white yet refreshingly cool interior, the eye is met by the most intricate inlaid-work* and ornamental design in the richest possible profusion, whilst around the openwork galleries, the cornice, the arches of the portals and windows, on the walls and along the entrance-passages, are inlaid, in black marble, verses of the Koran—the whole book, it is said, being thus reproduced in one part or other of the edifice.

In the centre of the vast marble rotunda, immediately beneath the lofty uprising dome, is an enclosure formed by a screen of trellis-work in marble, wrought in open tracery of the most intricate design. Where not carved upon, this marble is filled in with flowers of mosaic-work in precious stones, each flower being a very work of art in itself.† The cornelian, blood-stone, agate, and lapis lazuli, mostly prevail, and the flowers are apparently intended for the lotus, the iris, and the tulip, each flower of a like kind preserving the most faithful resemblance in colour, shape, and size. There are, in the joists of the doorway, at the entrance to the screen, iron supports, showing that it had originally doors. These

* It is in this building we first find that system of inlaying which became the chief characteristic of the style of the Moguls after the death of Akbar.

† In one flower I counted thirty different kinds of stones.

are stated to have been of solid silver studded with precious stones, and to have been worth one lac of rupees each. They were carried away when Agra was in possession of the Patans, at which time, as also probably subsequently, the building was plundered of such inlaid precious stones as are now found wanting in so many places. The so-called guardians of the place say that this latter spoliation was the work of our troops during the Mutiny; but this is quite improbable, at any rate to the extent to which the damage has been inflicted. It is far more likely that, after the wholesale plunder of the place by the Patans, a gradual system of robbery of the precious stones of the inlaid work of this and other buildings in the Upper Provinces was practised by the very natives placed in charge of them. Else, whence do the itinerant manufacturers of marble ornaments at Agra and elsewhere procure the stones (identical with those observable in the Taj) with which their wares are so curiously inlaid? That they *pay* for them, the price at which the manufactured articles are sold and the known dishonesty of the low-caste native forbid us to believe for one moment.

Inside the octagonal screen just described are the outer sarcophagi of Shah Jehan and Noor Jehan—the actual tombs being in a marble vault immediately beneath the building. They are of the purest marble, such as is said to be now unobtainable, and are profusely inlaid with precious stones, as is also the marble floor on which they stand. The tombs of the emperor and his wife lie side by side, but the former is higher than the latter.*

Our party had during this inspection of the place been talking somewhat loudly, and the echoes of the voices were rolling in harsh reverberations round and about the lofty dome. But having heard much of the effect of the echo as produced by *whispered* tones, I sang a few notes of the scale very gently, and then realized most fully the true effect as it had been described. The notes soared above, increasing in power, and repeating themselves in delicious melody until they gradually faded away, but yet so gradually that you doubted whether or

* The following is inscribed (in Persian) on this tomb:—"The magnificent tomb of the King, inhabitant of the two heavens, Ridwan and Khool; the most sublime sitter on the throne in Illeeyn (the starry heaven), dweller in Firdos (paradise) Shahjehan Badsha Gazee, peace to his remains: heaven is for him; his death took place the 26th day of Rujub in the year 1076 of the Hijree (1665 A.D). From this transitory world eternity has carried him off to the next."

not the sound had really departed. I then sang the 1st, 3rd, and 5th notes of the gamut in slow succession. The percussion of the octave from the first tone, and the blending of the whole into the full chord, as the notes ascended high aloft, was in effect something angelic and marvellous. It seemed as if a chorus of harmonies was being chanted above in strains of exquisite purity and softness; and I listened entranced and amazed at the wondrous effect, which, though I had partly anticipated it, surpassed my most sanguine expectations. I see it stated, in a Persian translation of a description of the Taj, that even unimaginative persons have been known to burst into tears on entering the building. Without going so far as this, I may truly assert that, to view this wondrous and exquisite structure, to stand beneath its high-arched dome, and to listen to the harmonies as they sweetly prolong themselves into strains of heavenly similitude around the marble vault, without becoming impressed, in the highest sense of the term, alike with the calm, serene loveliness of the spot and its associations, and with the grandeur and scope of the conception, one must be utterly insensible to the finer emotions of art and beauty. Indeed, as has been truly said, the sound under the dome is to the ear what the building is to the eye.

Descending a flight of polished marble steps immediately outside the entrance, and preceded by a torch-bearer, we now inspected the actual tomb of Shah Jehan and his beautiful queen,* which is a spacious vaulted chamber all of marble. The cenotaphs are also of marble, profusely inlaid with precious stones, and in-

* The Taj was erected by Shah Jehan to the memory of Noor Jehan (the Light of the World), his favourite queen, who died in child-birth, and who is reputed to have been a woman of surpassing beauty. It was commenced in 1630 A.D., and is said to have taken seventeen years to complete, and to have cost upwards of three millions sterling, notwithstanding that the labour of the 20,000 workmen employed on it was compulsory, and not paid for. In the Persian translation before referred to, a detailed description is given of the number of cart-loads of the marble and the various precious stones used in its construction, and of their individual cost. But although much of this, together with the names of the principal artists employed, is engraved in Persian in various parts of the building, it is highly probable the cost was not noted to a very great nicety, if we consider the proneness of Orientals to exaggerate. It may, however, be well conceived that an incalculable sum of money was expended in its erection; and as to the length of time it occupied, one might credit that almost any number of years had been required to elaborate its marvellously-intricate detail of ornamentation. A Frenchman, named Austin de Bordeux, is reputed to have been the architect. He was called by the natives Oostan Eesau, Nadir ol Asur—the Wonderful of the Age.

scribed with Persian characters. There is no light in this lower chamber but that which enters from the opening of the steps leading to it, and thus the reflected rays fall directly upon the marble tombs, greatly increasing the solemnity of the effect. The chamber, but for this borrowed light, would be in perfect darkness.

After sating our gaze with the never-ending beauties of the work around us, we left the building and ascended one of the minarets on the upper terrace, before described. As may be imagined, the view from this height is one of great extent and variety, and the river below is seen winding along an almost interminable track in silvery brightness, fringed by a yellow margin overflowed at intervals by the Jumna, which again is refreshingly bordered by brightly-green cultivated fields and topes of mango and bamboo.

Not satisfied with having seen the Taj in the light of the sun, we had resolved to see it also by night, illuminated by blue-lights. Of the effect of this, which is said to be so much greater than that by day, I can only say that it is worth observing from the contrast it affords to the more usual and natural method of inspection; but I cannot say that the result is, on the whole, so suggestive.* It is certainly different. Standing midway down the long garden walk (the best point of view), we witnessed, by the brilliant illumination of blue-lights from the minarets and terraces, the exquisite outline of the building, thrown into striking relief by the dark sky beyond, rendering the scene almost fairy-like in character, as, in an instant, with the extinguishing of the blue-lights, the building vanished as it were from view. I felt that it would have been truly a loss to have left Agra without this aspect of the wondrous Taj.

I found myself so knocked up with the visit I have just described as to render it impracticable to do any more sight-seeing that day; and, returning to the hotel, amused myself with an inspection of the curiosities which a crowd of itinerant vendors were eagerly waiting to display. They consisted of the famed soap-stone carvings and inlaid-work in marble and stone;

* The crowd of Mussulmen who hang about the building seem to drive a thriving trade in the sale of these blue-lights, for which they charge a sum of 8 annas (1s.) apiece. They also make a rich harvest from the presents of the many visitors to the Taj, who, as usual, are absurdly profuse in rewarding the crowd of hangers-on for no possible service rendered. The "guardians" seem thus truly to be able to realize and to enjoy the perfection of native happiness—doing nothing.

the former comprising baskets, flower-holders, platters, models of the Taj and other places; and the latter, paper-knives, miniature models of tombs, paper-weights, &c.

The soap-stone is a bluish-white material, remarkably soft and somewhat oily. It is found plentifully in the adjacent parts, and is easily susceptible of the most complex manipulation with the graver. Some of the carvings exhibited were really marvellous specimens of patient skill, and extremely light and graceful in design.

I was so pleased with one or two specimens, and considered them intrinsically so well worth the price asked, that I was about to offer the vendor *nearly half* what he demanded. A brother "Mason" who just then "made himself known," restrained me; and I thus secured some charming specimens for a price which I could not help thinking far less than their mere labour worth. The vendors, however, most readily offered any quantity at the same rate—so I conclude they were quite satisfied.

I have a very strong impression, as regards the inlaid-work, that the precious stones are plundered, as before suggested, from the public buildings. It is impossible otherwise to understand how the articles can be sold for the price they are. An exquisitely inlaid marble paperweight, ornamented with a beautiful floral design, in a dozen different stones most cunningly grouped and fitted, was offered for *four shillings;* whereas the workmanship alone must have cost almost that sum, taking labour at the lowest remunerative estimate.

It may have been very wrong, under these suspicious circumstances, to have purchased; but I am not ashamed to confess that I bought a good many specimens, and was very proud of my bargain. It is not every one, however, who is so fortunate in the matter of economy of prices. Displaying my treasures to some travellers whom I met shortly after, they assured me they had paid exactly *four times* the price which I had given for *precisely* the same articles. *Ergo:* if you are "a Brother of the Mystic Tie," always in travelling "discover yourself;" and you may be as fortunate in securing the good offices of a friend in this and many other respects, as I was.

The following day we set out to visit the Fort at Agra—a place the very sight of which impresses one with a just idea of the power and wealth of its founder.

Externally it is most imposing, with its massive but not ungraceful red, machicolated battlements 60 feet in height from the fosse, built in huge blocks of sand-stone. Against modern artillery, doubtless, these walls, which have stood so bravely the wear of three centuries, would be of little protection, but at the time of its erection it was manifestly a place of enormous strength, and the arrangement of its traverses, its covered causeways, its passages, and inner bastions—every approach commanded and covered by guns at all points—all show that the engineers of those days were not slightly skilled in the art of fortification. But it is rather of the objects of interest in the fort itself than of its aspect as a fortress, that I attempt a description.

The Fort, which is a mile and a half in circuit, contains the arsenal, Akbar's palace, and the celebrated Motee Musjid, or Pearl Mosque. In the centre of the Fort is a noble court-yard, 500 feet by 370, surrounded by arcades, and approached at the opposite ends through a succession of beautiful courts, opening into one another by gateways of great magnificence. On one side stands the building now used as an arsenal—a noble hall; and, filled as it now is, presenting a highly imposing appearance with its glittering array of tastefully arranged arms and flags, many of which have seen hard service. It was once the *dewan* or throne room of the Emperor Akbar, and measures 208 feet by 76, the roof being supported by three ranges of arches of great beauty. No unfit accompaniment of the fallen glories around, are the celebrated gates of Somnath, carried off by Lord Ellenborough, at the taking of Ghuznee in the invasion of Affghanistan.* The gates are entirely of sandal-wood, elaborately carved and inlaid; but they have suffered much from the ravages of time and change; and bear very plain evidence of repair by other than their original makers. In the centre of the Arsenal is also the marble throne or judgment-seat of Akbar. It has been once beautifully inlaid with jasper, cornelian, and other precious stones, but has suffered much from the depredations of its spoilers at various times.

Beyond the Arsenal, overlooking the Jumna, is the Emperor's palace, which is still in admirable preservation. In the Emperor's pavilion, where stands an exquisitely carved marble screen, the passage ruthlessly made by a cannon-

* Somnath was a holy Brahminical city near Goojrat, at the taking and sack of which by Mahmoud (A.D. 1001), he carried away to Ghuznee the splendid gates as a memorial of his victory. Mahmoud has the credit of being the first Mahomedan prince who established a solid power in India.

shot is visible; but whether at the time of the mutiny, or previous thereto, I could not with certainty learn. The precious stones forming the inlaid work of the pavilion have been barbarously mutilated and plundered; but enough still remain to attest the richness and beauty of the original design and the lavishness of execution. There is in the galleries, the balconies, and the corridors, a perfect forest of carving and ornamentation—marble, in the hands of the artists of those days, seeming tractable as wood, and capable of as florid ornamentation.

Perhaps the greatest curiosity of the place is the Shish-Mehal, or Hall of Glass. This is a chamber intended as a bath, covered over its entire surface with thousands of pieces of crystal arranged in the most intricate designs. In the centre is a marble basin, with cascades of marble leading from the wall. There is no direct light into the room; but that which is reflected from without is sufficient to illuminate this most fairy-like chamber, lighting up, in every tint of the rainbow, its thousands of mirror-like crystal squares. The effect of the room as lit up with coloured lamps, and with the waters gushing, sparkling, and plashing down from the tiny "falls," must have truly realized even the storied wonders of the "Arabian Nights."

Marble basins in which innumerable fountains once threw their cooling spray, are seen in great numbers in the various courts of the palace—in the floors of some of which are sunk channels for the water, the cooling effect of which must have been most enchanting. This is more so especially in the Zenana, from which a charming view of the City and the river is obtained.

Noticeable among the buildings of the Zenana is one devoted to the Emperor's Hindoo wives and attendants. This differs most materially in its architecture from the rest of the buildings in the Fort, and is distinguished by a special massiveness of structure without that lightness and variety of relief so strongly pervading the more pure Saracenic style. It is, however, extremely rich in its stone carvings, and will repay the closest inspection, and will startle by its minuteness of detail.

In one of a series of bomb-proof chambers (said to have been the sleeping-apartment of the Emperor), near the Zenana, is shown the room where Sir Russell Colvin died during the siege of the Fort by the rebels in 1858. His tomb, erected by his wife, is a prominent object on the arsenal green. Close adjoining lies the garden, with its fountains, its roses, its sweet scented trees, and tesselated court-yard of black and white marble, where the Emperor's favorite game of pachisi was wont to be played.*

The remaining principal object of interest is the Motee Musjid or Pearl Mosque, which may be considered one of the purest in style of all. It is an exquisitely beautiful building, surmounted by three domes, the interior being divided into as many aisles by a triple row of finely-proportioned Saracenic marble arches. Here is a culmination of refinement in taste and purity in execution which is in grateful contrast to some of the more gorgeous decorations of the palace.

A survey of the lavishly ornamented and costly buildings within this truly martial and regal abode convinces one that their founder, whatever may have been his failings, possessed a deep appreciation of the grand and beautiful in Art. He was, indeed, one of the greatest builders of his race; in evidence of which he has left more traces and remembrances of his name and power than any other Indian monarch.

* For a description of this game, see *post.*

The town of Agra itself, as seen after a visit to the Fort, is meagre in the extreme. Since the Mutiny, vast clearances of buildings have been made, and as the remains of these still lie in many a heap over the city, the effect, as may be imagined, is none of the finest; added to which there seem few if any buildings about the palace equal to the average even of large Indian cities. Whether Agra will ultimately be converted into the cleanly and orderly city that Lucknow is now, is a thing to be doubted, but nevertheless hoped for.

Our next place of visit now was Futtehpore Sikree. This place is so named from the villages of Futtehpore and Sikree, which lie on either side, and was erected by the Emperor Akbar, in 1571, as a summer residence for himself and Court.

Having already hired a dâk (such as before described), we set out early in the morning, arriving at noon. The road is for the most part good, but fearfully dusty, from the fact that the traffic is principally with native hackeries, camels, and mules; and these intentionally (on account of the softness of the ground) keep on the soft *kucchha* road on either side of the metalled highway, raising a perpetual cloud of dust.

Toiling up a steep ascent lined on either side with stony ruin, we found ourselves in a large open quadrangle, having a pile of red sand-stone buildings on two of its sides, and a smaller structure of the same material on the third. This, we found, was the dwelling used as a dâk bungalow. True to the instincts of Englishmen, we at once gave orders to the *Khanamah* in attendance to prepare a tiffin of grilled fowl, eggs, and chupatties * by our return. We then set forth, under the auspices of a well-to-do looking Mussulman, who presented himself as a guide, to view these celebrated ruins, the scattered remains of which lay around for some six miles in circumference.

On proceeding into the interior, and beholding the vast structures before me, I was struck as much by their excellent state of preservation as by their extent and grandeur. Built in blocks of red sand-stone—resembling coarse granite, for the most part of immense size, they seemed impervious alike to time and change; and in their massive but barbaric grandeur resembled Egyptian remains rather than those of a Mussulman dynasty.

* Travellers need to bring their own beer, tea, or soda water with them.

It would be difficult adequately to describe, in detail, all the labyrinth of courts, pavilions, and palaces in which the ruins abound. I will content myself, therefore, with explaining the principal objects of interest, adding such other information respecting them as I was enabled to gather from our loquacious guide, who spoke with an authoritativeness such as might have led one to suppose he had been an eye-witness of all he described.

Ascending a flight of steps, and passing a gateway of colossal size, you enter a vast marble court-yard, measuring 428 by 406 feet, in which are several basins of water where once fountains gaily sparkled. The glare from the sun on the brilliant and polished marble pavement is so intense that you gladly seek a cooler location under the shelter of a lofty-pillared, marble-paved corridor of most graceful proportions, which runs almost round the court-yard. At one end of this court is another magnificent gateway, rising in a series of terraces to a height of 120 feet, flanked on each side by an elegant tripled dome mosque.* An ascent to the top

* On the door of this gateway are nailed several horse-shoes; our guide, in reply to inquiries on the subject, stated that they had been taken from the feet of horses who were sick, and no sooner was the shoe nailed there "than the animal immediately recovered."

of this gateway is usually made. A wide view is afforded from its summit of the surrounding plain, dotted with its villages; on the left can just be discerned the spires of the palace of Bhurtpore, some twenty miles distant, while to the right the pure white dome of the Taj looms faint but distinct as the sun is seen glittering on its marble roof.

At the foot of a deep flight of stone steps of enormous width are seen the remains of the Baths of the palace, but there is nothing in them worthy of note. On the right of the court-yard, facing some marble Tombs in the open court, is the Durgah or Tomb of Sheik Selim —a holy man through whose intervention, or in accordance with whose predictions, tradition asserts, Jehanghir, the son of Akbar, was born. The Emperor, out of gratitude for this service, showered fortune and honour on the saint while he lived, and on his death built this superb shrine. Indeed, tradition asserts that the building of Futtehpore Sikree itself is attributable to the fact of its having been the abode of the Sheikh. The tomb is approached by a marble porch, having at the corners a curious massive ornament, resembling somewhat the letter *S*. Before the entrance is a marble screen of the most elaborate carving—more elaborate, I think, than that at the Taj itself. Interiorly, the fairy-like lightness, elegance, and beauty of proportion, the flowery carvings on the pillars, and the marble filagree work abounding, are things that surpass the most extravagant expectation, and almost defy description.

Inside, covering the tomb itself, is a gracefully arched canopy, six feet in height, covered with mother-of-pearl, rivetted in small pieces with brass pins; dazzlingly rich and brilliant, as, lit up by the reflected rays of the sun from the outside shining marble court, the refracted light appears in all the colours of the rainbow. The floor is of jasper, and the walls of pure white marble, inlaid with cornelian, onyx, and jasper; the doors of the shrine being of solid carved ebony.

Our guide, on entering, reverently left his slippers at the entrance, but did not seem (so degenerate is the age) to expect us to follow his example: nor did we. We found a crimson cloth covered over the marble tomb under the inlaid canopy, and being curious to know if there was aught to be seen beneath, begged our guide to upraise it. He, however, protested against this, though unable to assign any reason for his objection; and we therefore insisted on having the cloth removed, seeing that even any outward form of reverence to the place has long since been considered unnecessary. Nothing was visible except the usual form of marble tomb. Questioning the guide as to his own particular post at the ruins, he informed us that he *was a direct descendant of the Sheik;* and that his (the guide's) great grandfather lay buried fronting the mosque, where several marble sarcophagi are seen placed near together. These he described as being all near relatives of Saint Selim. He stated that some thirty persons, he being the chief, were retained to take care of the place. The ruins themselves, he professed, belonged to, and were under the control of, Government, who allowed a sum of 6,000 rupees a year for their repair. But the Nawab who claimed to inherit them (a descendant also of the saint) had received from Government a grant of the tomb and its belongings, on which he spent a considerable yearly sum. At the time of our visit, indeed, a new roof of pure marble was being put to the mosque by the Nawab, at a cost, our guide stated, of 10,000 rupees.

Adjoining the Tomb of the Sheik is a lofty and superbly carved and decorated Hall, paved with marble and supported on rows of giant pillars. At one side is a raised marble throne, and this probably was used as an Audience Chamber. It is in sufficiently good repair to answer the like purpose now, were such required.

Descending to a slightly lower elevation, we found ourselves facing the Palace of the Rajah Beer Buhl, Akbar's Prime Minister. It has a cupolated roof, and is built entirely of red sandstone, being in almost as perfect preservation as on the day it was first constructed. The rooms are somewhat small, but are adorned with a profusion of carving, exciting wonderment as to the length of time and the number of artists who must have been engaged upon it. There is scarcely an inch of uncarved stone in the whole building; and indeed all the edifices partake, to a great degree, of the same elaborate and laborious ornamentation. In this building certain rooms are kept "furnished" for the use of visitors, who have the option of residing here for a few days on paying a small fee. Shade of Akbar! How little did the royal founder of the pile imagine that any part of his palace would be thus desecrated.

Akbar, who has the credit of having been a liberal-minded man in the matter of religion, built not only distinctive residences for his Mussulman and Hindoo wives, but one also for a

Christian woman, named Marie, whom he "married." This building adjoins the Emperor's Palace and the Zenana, and, unlike the other structures, is ornamented with paintings in fresco. The Greek cross is also in many places decipherable; and on one side are two tablets, now much disfigured, one of which, however, is still sufficiently distinct to confirm the generally considered opinion that it may have been intended for the "Annunciation."

Close to the Belatee Beebee's (English Lady's) palace, as our guide termed it, is the Panch Mehal (or five-storied house). It consists of a series of terraces, rising one above the other pyramidally to a considerable height, the lower platform being supported by richly carved pillars. This was probably used by the Emperor and his wives as a place of retreat in the cool of the morning and evening, whence, surveying the scene around, they were enabled to breathe from this elevation the freshened air.

In a courtyard beyond is shown the Emperor's Pachisi-board,* composed of large slabs

* The following account of this now obsolete game is taken from a sketch published in an old Agra periodical:—

"The game is usually played by four persons, each of whom is supplied with four wooden or ivory cones, which are called 'gots,' and are of different colours for distinction. Victory consists in getting these four pieces safely through of parti-coloured sandstone, each square sufficiently large for a person to stand or sit on. In one corner of this courtyard is a most singular labyrinthine building, said to have been used by the ladies of the Zenana as a place wherein to amuse themselves with the game of "hide and seek."

We now come to the Dewan-i-Khass, or Council Chamber of the Emperor, a building of most eccentric design. Though externally two stories are seen, on entrance the second story is found to consist only of a quadrangular stone causeway, starting from and resting on a centre massive pillar, elaborately carved. Round the wall runs a circular balcony, communicating with each of the four angles

all the squares of each rectangle into the vacant place in the centre—the difficulty being, that the adversaries take up in the same way as pieces are taken up at backgammon. Moving is regulated by throwing 'cowries,' whose apertures falling uppermost or not, affect the amount of the throw by certain fixed rules. But on this Titanic board of Akbar's wooden or ivory 'gots' would be lost altogether. Sixteen girls, therefore, dressed distinctively—say four in red, four in blue, four in white, four in yellow—were trotted up and down the squares, taken up by an adversary, and put back at the beginning again; and at last, after many difficulties, four of the same colour would find themselves giggling into their dopattas together in the middle space, and the game was won."

which radiate from the centre pillar. The signification of this curious design is explained to be, that Akbar, seated thus aloft in the centre of the Council Hall, received from his four Ministers, stationed at each of the four angles, advice, as from the four quarters of the globe—himself, the centre of power and authority, issuing also thence his commands to all parts of the world.

On the East of the Dewan-i-Khass is the Dewan-i-Amm, from the balcony of which it was the custom of the Emperor to make his first daily public appearance.

In the same Court is a Pavilion erected for another saint—only one of the *Hindoo* religion—a Gooroo, and occupied by him during his lifetime. The architecture of this building is much less Saracenic in character than the others,—probably out of regard to the feelings of the occupant. The roof is of great height, pyramidal in form, and elaborately carved and ornamented.

On a terrace lower down are the stables for the Emperor's stud, a lengthy and massively-built stone range, affording accommodation for 250 horses. The iron rings to which the horses were fastened, and their stone eating-troughs, are still almost as intact as when used by neighing steeds some 300 years ago.

A little further down the hill, on the north side of the palace of Beer-Buhl, is a large gate called the Elephant Gate. At the bottom of the hill is also a tower, some 90 feet high, termed the *Hatti-minar.* It is studded with elephants' tusks, and presents a most curious appearance. Its origin is scarcely known, but it is probable that it may have been erected in memory of some favourite elephant.

Thoroughly exhausted with our inspection of the labyrinth of courts, pavilions, and palaces, we were not sorry to seek the shelter of the Dâk Bungalow, formerly the Dufter-khana, or office, of the Court. It is built of large blocks of sandstone, but, except in point of massiveness of construction, there is no especial feature worthy of remark.

The tongue of our guide had hardly ceased going during a three-hours' inspection of these ruins, and much of the information he desired to impart was lost by the parrot-like way in which he gabbled forth his tale, being apparently unable to answer a direct question unless he took up his narrative again at a particular point. We rewarded the man for his trouble with a present of a rupee, at which he murmured greatly, having, as he intimated, received as much as a gold mohur, (16 Rs.) from "many Sahibs." We thereupon asked for the rupee to be given back, when he at once professed himself delighted beyond measure with the liberality of the gift; thus still further illustrating the remarks made in a previous chapter on the subject of "Bucksheesh" to natives. Having duly refreshed ourselves at the Bungalow, we slowly descended the hill on our return journey, deeply impressed with a sense of the grandeur and magnificence of the ruins of Futtehpore Sikree.

It is objected by some that the remains of the mighty structures erected by the Mahometan rulers of Hindostan are devoid of interest from the great similarity in style. Similar they are, it is true; but I think it will be found that each possesses special claims and merits of its own; and the historian or the traveller will add greatly to his knowledge and to his pleasure by a careful study and comparison of their several specialities. The buildings of Akbar are almost invariably of red sandstone, elaborately wrought. Those of Shah Jehan, on the other hand, are mostly of marble, whilst the structures of the Patans are celebrated for a wondrous massiveness of construction, combined with an exquisite elaboration of detail. Indeed, it is said of them that they built like giants, and finished like goldsmiths.

Akbar was hardly fourteen years old when he ascended the throne, and he reigned fifty-one years. His mausoleum, already mentioned as one of the celebrities of Agra, is situate about eight miles from the town. It stands in a spacious garden, and is a splendid building of sandstone, with upper stories of marble. The entrance to the grounds is by four gateways, seventy feet high, leading on to as many stone causeways, converging to a stone platform 400 feet square, on which the edifice proudly uprises.

The remains of the Emperor lie in the vaults below, and are covered in the centre hall by a plain slab of marble, as in the other mausoleums noticed, but above is another slab similar to the one beneath, on which are inscribed the *nau nubbee nām*, or ninety-nine attributes of Allah. Protecting this is a gilded dome, the mausoleum else being open to the sky. The general character of the building is more florid in style and more profusely brilliant in decoration, than usual; but the general magnificence of the structure, with its airy cupolas, its rich contrast of marble and sandstone, and its imposing approaches, perpetuates no less the affection of its builder, Jehangir, than the greatness of him in honour of whose memory it was erected.

CHAPTER VIII.

AGRA TO DELHI.

Shahjehanabad—The English position during the Siege—The Fort—The Chandney Chowk—Appearance of the Town—The Jumna Musjid—A Native Wedding—Specialities of Delhi Manufacture—Hawkers of Delhi—Delhi Conjurors—Tomb of Sufder Jung—Dwellers in Tombs—Novel Diving—The Kootub—Humayoon's Tomb—Old Delhi—Climate of Delhi—Native Women.

HAVING now seen all of interest in Agra, we set off by the early morning train for Delhi, arriving at about noon. The station is at present a temporary structure; but as soon as the bridge, now in course of erection across the Jumna, is completed, a handsome terminus will be built here, although, to the great chagrin of the inhabitants, Delhi will remain but a loop line, the rail running, for its *direct* length, from Gazeeabad to Meerut, which will henceforth take precedence of Delhi as a military depôt. Thus Shahjehanabad, the proud and magnificent; the spot made famous by the poets of Hindustan; the place from whence, in the days of its splendour, issued the devastating armies of the Moguls; containing, too, on its site the ruins of ten cities of the same name, is destined to subside into a second-rate town, no longer even to be distinguished as the head-quarters of a regiment.

The sites of its former towns, at different epochs, extend some 10 miles to the south-east and south-west. More or less over this large extent of ground lie scattered the wrecks of palaces, forts, graveyards, tombs—palaces in themselves—and all the evidences of former greatness—greatness such as we in the 19th century cannot even boast of ability or means to imitate. Many of these ruins are still in a sufficiently good state of preservation to attest the lavishness of expenditure and the endurance of construction which, after the lapse of so many centuries, has almost earned for them the reputation of indestructibility; and as each successive conqueror came, he seems to have sought to excel his predecessors in works of grandeur and majesty.*

An old writer thus describes Delhi as it appeared in 1835:—" From the outside the view is splendid; domes and mosques, cupolas and minarets, with the imperial palace forming like a mountain of red granite, appear in the midst of groves of clustering trees, so thickly planted that the buildings have been compared, in oriental imagery, to rocks of pearls and rubies, rising from an emerald sea. In approaching the city from the east bank of the Jumna, the prospect realizes all that the imagination has pictured of oriental magnificence, mosques and minarets glittering in the sun, some garlanded with wild creepers, others arrayed in all the pomp of gold, the exterior of the cupolas being covered with brilliant metal; and from Mount Mejnoon, over which a fine road now passes, the shining waters of Jumna, gleaming in the distance, insulating Selimgurh and disappearing behind the halls of the peacock-throne, the palace of the Emperors, add another beautiful feature to the scene." But, alas! thirty years have wrought

* Delhi has been captured, sacked, destroyed, and rebuilt, on different sites no less than eleven times, the importance of its position rendering its restoration each time a necessity.

a wondrous change, and although Delhi is undoubtedly a fine city—now rendered cleanly and cheerful looking, the visitor will suffer a shock to feelings romantic when comparing the departed glories of this once celebrated place with its present more utilitarian aspect.

The approach to the famed capital of the Moslem Kings is, however, still most imposing. The city, brightly shining with many gilded domes and cupolas, and thickly embowered with tall spreading trees, stands proudly in the centre of a sandy plain, flanked on the one side by the ruins of old Delhi. The mighty Jumna flows in its front.* The green valley of the Punjab lies on its right, while in the rear rises a range of sandstone rocks, near which are situated, for the most part, the European dwellings of the place.

The entire city proper is enclosed by a low machicolated rampart, with massive bastions approached through eight noble fortified entrances, termed the Cashmere, Moree, Cabul, Lahore, Ajmere, Turkoman, Delhi, and Calcutta gates.

On a range of sandstone rocks to the right,

* At the foot of the ruins of *old* Delhi, the Jumna also once flowed, and the city seems thus to have followed the course of the river, as it changed.

termed the Ridge, is Hindoo Rao's house, from whence the best view of the city is obtainable. This was occupied by a party of European troops, during the siege in 1857; and close by is the commencement of a building (called by the natives "Futtey Ghur"), which appears designed as a memorial of the siege. The Ridge was then the centre of the English position. North of it, and near the Jumna, were the parade-ground and British lines. There is nothing worthy of note in the building itself, nor of particular interest as regards its former occupant, who was compelled to take shelter in Delhi from the design entertained against his life. His sister managed to effect his escape, and subsequently provided for him in the most liberal manner. The edifice is now undergoing repair for occupation as a hospital for European troops, the site being perhaps one of the best and healthiest in Delhi.

From this high ground in the rear of the city, during the protracted siege in 1857, our troops advanced to the assault, being in the main part located here. Mounting the signal tower in its midst, the parallels of the besieging force and plan of the final attack are clearly understood, and the Cashmere Gate is seen which the 52nd Light Infantry so gallantly and successfully assaulted on that occasion. The brave exploits of Lieuts. Salkell and Home, with their small party of sappers, will be long remembered: they having, in the face of a murderous musketry fire from the walls, which destroyed in great part their gallant band, attached a bag of gun-powder to the gate, and so blown it to pieces.

Very early in the morning after our arrival we set out to "see the lions." Our first visit was to the Fort, situated on the edge of the Jumna, which although in the hot season is little better than a canal or series of canals, swells, in the freshes, to a mighty rushing stream, one or two miles broad. The Fort is approached by two grand portals—the Lahore Durwaza, and the Delhi Durwaza; the former with its covered stone arcade, 500 feet long, and of proportionate height, being justly considered the finest structure of the kind in the world. Running parallel with these gates is an embattled wall of red granite, sixty feet high, enclosing the Fort. Besides the noble and secure approaches described, the Fort has a third on the opposite bank of the river, over a low stone bridge, flanked by a fortified work, gloomy in its grim strength, called Selim-gurh (the house of Selim), which has played its part, both as prison and fortress, in the troublous wars of the Moguls.

The interior of the Fort now presents a mean, dismantled, and wretched appearance. Its buildings were principally devoted to the use of the King and his court; and the remains of the Palace and Hall of Audience, although now shorn of their grandeur, and partly in ruins, attest the lavish decoration and beauty of the renowned "Seat of the Moguls."

The Dewan-i-Khass, or Hall of Audience, is now used as a museum, and is filled with a most interesting collection of oriental curiosities, antique Eastern arms and chain armour, models, geological specimens and instructive drawings, the King's throne, and much else of value and interest to the curious.

The Hall is divided, as it were, into a smaller inner chamber by a series of massive square marble pillars, around the cornice of which is the inscription, quoted by Moore, in his "Lalla Rookh":—

"If there be a paradise on earth, it is this, it is this."

The whole of the interior has been very richly ornamented with gold arabesque; and the roof (originally of silver) and pillars are still so decorated. At the entrance of the Museum is the ball and cross of St. Paul's Church, which was so ruthlessly injured by the rebels in 1857 as to necessitate its being taken down. There it stands, riddled with bullet holes, a notable evidence of the kind of respect paid by the fanatical Mahometan to the emblem of our faith. The external appearance of the Dewan-i-Khass is not in its favour, resembling, as it now does, a barrack more than anything else. Originally, however, it was open on its four sides, and the sloping marble eaves of the roof projected over richly-carved, wide-spreading Moorish arches.

Leaving the Fort, you find yourself in a broad, cleanly-looking road, along which we will pass, and diverge into the town itself. Traversing some narrow streets, crowded with busy people, and lined by the funniest of shops, gaily painted, and at this early hour of the morning well filled with customers, we emerge presently into *the* thoroughfare of Delhi —the Chandney Chowk. Here the shops present a very improved appearance over the generality of native bazaars, and there is a manifest air of well-to-doism prevailing. Extending nearly its entire length is an avenue of fine shady trees, and on either side are several buildings, very pretentious in point of decorative art; the cornices and walls being raised in rich arabesque stuccoed relief, and ornamented with floral designs in pigment. But the decoration is necessarily of very temporary duration, and needs frequent renewal. The majority of the houses and shops, however, are unornamented, and of a most heterogenous character, as much so in their outer appearance as in the nature of their contents, which embrace every known oriental art-manufacture; their neatly-clothed turbaned owners outside, beseeching (in Parsee-English) an inspection of their wares, and playing no unimportant part in the general picturesqueness and effect of the scene.

Most of the houses have shallow projecting balconies of a highly insecure appearance, in which, in the cool of the evening, the native "merchant," or shop-keeper, and his family may be seen enjoying their *otium* over a *hubble-bubble*, and clad in the most invitingly cool deshabille of white flowing muslin.

But it is not by a glance at the clean and orderly Chandney Chowk—the boulevards of Delhi—that an adequate idea of its multitudinous dwellings and inhabitants can be gained. You must penetrate behind the scene, and, passing under some one of the archways along the line of thoroughfare, grope your way through an intricacy of courts and alleys as numerous and perplexing as they are narrow and filthy. Here, in a city of itself, dwells a vast population, unseen, as it were, but as busy and apparently as healthy—strange to say—as the multitude in the more open and savoury part of the town.*

Since the Mutiny, crowded as it even now is, the native town has been much cleared away, and what remains but very imperfectly represents the extent or population of the place as it existed ten years ago. Especial attention has also been given to planting the city with trees, and many have already grown up, adding greatly to its appearance. When first planted, the trees are built round with a brick-work wall, to preserve them from the cattle, and the hundreds of these erections about the roads have a peculiar effect, at first sight giving the idea of so many wells.

* It is worthy of note, indeed, that Delhi is, as a rule, more healthy than the neighbouring stations of Meerut, Agra, Kurnaul, and Umballa, of which Agra is certainly the worst. A reference to the annual medical reports will satisfy the most sceptical on this point. Even epidemics visit Delhi in a much milder form than they do the other stations.

A noticeable feature in the town, running through its entire length, is the famous canal of Delhi. It was originally constructed by order of Feroze Shah, and then, and for a long time after, formed the only source from whence the inhabitants obtained wholèsome water. It subsequently fell into bad repair, became choked up, and its loss proved the cause of so much disease and suffering to the place, that in 1820 it was reconstructed, and finally, a few years ago, put into permanent order by the British Government. The water from whence this canal is supplied takes its rise from a very extensive jheel* some 20 miles from Delhi, the constant fresh-running stream from which conduces greatly to the health of the city, carrying away, as it does, in its flow the main refuse of the place, and supplying in its course the all necessary means of irrigation to the public gardens of the city.

Near the Chandney Chowk,. proudly overlooking the town, the Fort, and the surrounding country, stands the Jumna Musjid, the crowning work of Aurungzebe, and which is, *par excellence, the* Mahometan temple of India.

* This same jheel which supplies the reservoir, by being dammed up in a portion of its length, serves also as an irrigating canal for the adjacent country.

Built on the summit of a rock, it is approached on three sides by as many noble gateways, up an imposing pyramidal flight, some twenty feet in height, of thirty-seven stone steps. On this level, above the ground, is the platform on which the building commences. Approaching by the steps from the north, you find yourself opposite a handsome gateway of red sandstone. Its front is triangular; and above it is surmounted with a kind of gallery, faced with ornamental arches. On the roof of this gallery are fifteen small marble domes, close side by side, their spires tipped with gold; and above these, again, six fluted marble minarets, of unequal height, with open arched chambers at top and gilt pinnacles over all, rise gracefully against the sky.

The outer archway is forty feet high and pointed, and recedes inwards some six feet, curving gradually to the doorway, which is some sixteen feet high. To this are attached a pair of massive wooden doors, four inches thick, and overlaid half an inch in depth with solid brass, handsomely ornamented in arabesque design. Entering, you come at once into a stone chamber formed in the thickness of the gate, and intended as a guard chamber for those in charge of the precincts.* Passing through, you step into a vast quadrangle, 325 feet square, paved with stone flags, each flag being three feet square, in the centre of which is a marble basin and fountain. Round three sides of the court runs an open sandstone piazza, fifteen feet wide, with columns of same material, terminating in narrow arches, and adorned at each corner of its flat terrace roof with marble and gilt cupolas. The roof itself is composed of blocks of sandstone, each fifteen feet long by one and a half feet wide.

Fronting the East is the Motee Musjid, or Pearl Mosque, itself occupying nearly the whole of the fourth side of the square. You enter up a flight of marble steps by a lofty doorway with receding arch, the outer crown of which is eighty feet high by fifty wide, and the centre point of the doorway thirty feet high. The facing of the Musjid is sandstone and marble, the latter inlaid so as to form a design in relief, as it were, against the otherwise monotonous hue of the stone. And on large marble panels of the inlaid work is inscribed, in Arabic, the date of erection of the

* All the gateways of the time of Akbar and Shah Jehan are similar in construction in these and most other respects.

building, 1620; the name of its founder, Aurungzebe;? its cost, ten lacs of rupees; and the time it took in erecting, twelve years. At the corners of the Mosque rise two lofty minarets, 120 feet high, containing as many steps. These towers are inlaid throughout their whole height with flutings of white marble, and are surmounted with the usual graceful white marble cupolas. Vast as these noble minarets are in proportion, they yet look aërial and delicate in relation to the extent and grandeur of the whole structure.

Proceeding through the splendid doorway, before described, to the interior of the Mosque, fronting which is a marble pulpit on a platform of seven steps for the Imaum to call the faithful to prayer, you stand in a lofty hall eighty feet long, and wide in proportion, paved with large slabs of white marble inlaid with black. Spanning the width of the Hall, spring eight noble Saracenic arches of red sandstone inlaid with marble, the lower panels being entirely of the latter material. The vista here obtained is grand and imposing in the extreme.

In the Mosque reverently kneeling were only some half-dozen sedate-looking Mussulmen, but at the regular time of evening or morning prayer, or on any special occasion, it is no uncommon thing to find from 4,000 to 5,000 worshippers assembled at one time in the vast open court, earnestly engaged in a uniform but intent devotion.

Ascending one of the lofty minarets, a superb birds'-eye view is obtained of the town, with its teeming busy hive of men beneath. Most, if not all, the houses are puckka-built,* and you look down on a wilderness of terraced roofs and white walls, with here and there a patch of green, and many a graceful line of trees relieving the scene. Far off against the horizon rises gracefully the lofty Kootub Minar; the white dome of Humayoon's tomb, seen in the midst of a refreshingly green plain, glistens nearer in the sun; while the ruins of old Delhi, closer still, lie in fallen magnificence around.

Descending, and inquiring if there was aught else to be seen, our cicerone said that the greatest sight of all was yet in store—being no less than an illuminated MS. copy of the Koran, said to be 700 years old. Summoning an aged and venerable-looking priest, a door in an opposite building was unlocked, and from a carefully secured chest was withdrawn a parch-

* The term *puckka* signifies anything built entirely of stone, or of bricks and mortar.

ment volume enwrapped in folds of silk. The priest reverently opened the book, and seemed intensely disgusted at our want of reverence in attempting to handle it. The writing is in the Arabic character, and the colour of the ink, even now, a brilliant jet. It is certainly a fine specimen of penmanship, and might not unworthily find a place beside some of our black letter masterpieces of the olden time.

The Sheikh related that the holy book had been on one occasion taken possession of by an unscrupulous but powerful noble, who, however, on hearing that the worshippers and priests of the Musjid ceased not day and night to weep for and deplore its loss, graciously returned it. But I am told the real truth is, that at the time of the Mutiny it was removed by some careful rebel for safe keeping, and replaced, on the restoration by our Government of the Mosque to the Mussulmen. As we left the Mosque a Mussulman came in, and seeing the book, reverently kissed many times the cover which had contained it, and proceeded to outpour to the attendant priest some confession.

Returning from our visit to the Jumna Musjid, we witnessed the procession of a rich native wedding. We first received intimation of some special occasion being celebrated by finding our progress through the street completely impeded. In front approached an apparently interminable line of vehicles, people, and quadrupeds. First, a dozen equipages of every conceivable shape and variety, from the European-made gharry to the country araba, the latter gaily decorated with scarlet cloth, hung with jingling bells, and packed with white-robed Mussulmen, gaily sporting the brightest of scarfs and showiest of spangled caps. Then, a pair of gigantic black elephants in single file, with double-sided howdahs on their backs, in which were seated a group of young lads dressed in white, and covered with spangled scarfs, gold-embroidered slippers, and skull-caps. Next, a string of long-necked camels, tied together, the object of whose appearance, except for the purpose of ostentation, I was at a loss to divine. Now, a pair of boxes on poles, something between a palkee and a sedan-chair, in each of which was seated, cross-legged, a very fair-complexioned child, from about six to eight years old, looking supremely uncomfortable with the heap of clothing and ornaments with which it was encumbered. A lady who was with us immediately pronounced these children to be the bride and bridegroom, and so we thought until half a dozen similar youngsters (of which sex it was impossible accurately to guess) filed by; each sedan-chair, or whatever you please to call it, having in attendance on either side a swell *chuprassie*, or native servant, swinging a long chowrie, with which he assiduously swept away the flies and dust. A score of mounted gentry brought up the rear, dressed in all the colours of the rainbow, their steeds, no less gaily arrayed, proudly arching their necks with all the grace of the Arab, curvetting and prancing the while, as restrained by their riders with the evident desire of "showing off" their elegant paces. Behind followed a tagrag and bobtail of the most heterogeneous description; whilst in, around, and about the cavalcade marched musicians in groups of two and four, some banging mercilessly at brass gongs held aloft, while others kept up the very "devil's tattoo" on an oblong cone-shaped apparatus like a drum. They were accompanied by another musician on a sort of conch, a cross between a speaking trumpet and a bagpipe, but which for power and hideousness of sound left the others nowhere.

Imagine all this—the finery, the wealth, the dirt, the poverty, the crowd, the noise, the dust, the heat, the glare, and the attendant Babel from bystanders and exultant lookers-on —and you will have some idea, though even then an imperfect one, of the procession of a "rich" native wedding.

We were not a little glad to escape at last from the almost interminable throng, and, choked with dust, to seek the cool shelter of our hotel. We had no sooner arrived, than we were surrounded and literally besieged by a host of itinerant vendors of the specialities of Delhi, consisting of Cashmere cloths, Delhi embroidery, Delhi paintings, Cashmere shawls, Delhi jewellery, ivory carvings, and the like. Most of these vendors are proprietors of shops in the town, who endeavour thus to forestall a little business by displaying, uninvited, their wares, some of which will be found tempting enough.

Before you have time to forbid them, these men will have opened their linen bundles, and displayed before your now longing eyes the most exquisite fabrics in every colour of the rainbow, covered with the finest embroidery in braid, in gold, in silver thread, and silk. Opera cloaks, scarfs, chogas (a kind of loose dressing-gown for gentlemen), ravishing Cashmere shawls, rare and rich enough to tempt the most self-denying of ladies, ivory and sandal wood carvings, wondrous miniature paintings on ivory,* of the softest and finest finish—by these, and I know not what else, you find yourself surrounded; and woe be to your purse if you be not deaf to the seductions laid for you.

These hawkers must drive a splendid trade with the visitors who pass through Delhi, getting, as they do, on the average, double the real value for their goods. At any rate, their appearance is indicative of considerable prosperity; for nowhere will you see such well-clothed, and, in every respect, well-to-do looking natives. The prices asked by these itinerants, in the first instance, are, of course, very different from what is gladly taken after half an hour's bargaining; but it is, nevertheless, a very unsafe method of purchase, since the fact of your getting an article for half the price first demanded is by no means a surety that you have got it cheap. These rascals are now so cunning, and so well conversant with our system of "beating down," that they ask in proportion, and it is thus very difficult to know whether one has made a bargain or

* Miniature painting on ivory is said to have been introduced into Delhi, some fifty years ago, by an English lady.

not. There are, however, one or two very respectable shops in the Chandney Chowk, where the prices asked are, within a small margin, the fair market value, and to these, if the traveller really is in search of genuine articles, he should go direct. For instance, we were shown shawls, the price of which asked was 2,000 rupees, and we bought the same (with but little bargaining) at the shop for 800 rupees.

Whilst occupied with an army of these hawkers, a troupe of native conjurors made their appearance; and as Delhi is famous for the skill of these people, I was glad to have an opportunity of seeing a performance. Permission was therefore at once accorded for the show to commence; whereupon half a dozen almost nude natives cleared a space for themselves in a corner of the room, and squatting down in their own approved method, commenced quite a fire of words in the vernacular. Their entire apparatus was contained in a small canvas bag, and consisted of a few bowls, pipes, boxes, and wicker baskets, most rude in construction, and certainly not suggestive of any marvellous mechanism. Yet with these helps, our conjurors went through a most astonishing series of tricks, some of which would baffle Colonel Stodare himself. Not to speak of performing serpents appearing from empty snake-skins, and the host of ordinary tricks exhibited by most itinerant jugglers, we witnessed the growth of a mango-tree from a seed; the swallowing of baskets full of knives, nails, and tape; the drinking of a mixture of three powders—red, white, and blue—in a glass of water, and the production, immediately afterwards, from the operator's mouth, of each powder in a dry state, separately, and that after he had rinsed his mouth twice with clean water. What was done would have been sufficiently marvellous, even with the usual European appliances, but as performed by nude people, in the almost entire absence of mechanical contrivances, the display did infinite credit to the talent of these self-taught *prestidigitateurs;* and our English celebrities might evidently learn much from them.

A visit to the Jumna Musjid, the town and the fort, with visits from the hawkers and conjurors, I found ample occupation for one day; and the glare of the sun being very intense at Delhi, we set out for the next place of interest, the Kootub, some eight miles distant (situate twelve miles S.W. of Delhi), in the grey dawn of the next morning; taking a tiffin with us, and proposing to return in the cool of the evening.

Half-way on the road to the Kootub, on the right, is a large building, standing in a considerable enclosure of ground. This is the tomb of Sufder Jung, or as he was better known amongst his countrymen by the title of Abdool Munsoor Khan. He was a successful military adventurer, who played a prominent part in the troublous times antecedent to Mohammed Shah's ascent of the throne. Cramped with an hour's ride in a not over well-balanced gharry, we were very glad to alight and inspect the mausoleum. It is a vast structure, occupying the centre of a large enclosure. The building is of considerable architectural pretensions, and, notwithstanding the long lapse of years since its erection, it is even now in admirable preservation, attesting the solidity and permanence of the wondrous structures of the Moguls.

In two hours we arrived in full view of the Kootub, but directed our steps first, according to advice received, to some curious wells adjoining. The peculiarity of these wells is, that they are tank-shaped, being built in by large blocks of sand-stone; the descent to the water is by a series of three gradually widening platforms, nearly twenty feet apart, making a depth from the ground to the surface of the water of from fifty to sixty feet. The water (in February) was twenty feet deep, but in the rains it is forty feet. On our approach, half a dozen boys and men rushed up to the highest platform, and dived one after another, feet foremost, into the depths. On nearing the water, the legs and arms (which on first plunging had been extended) were brought close together, and the body disappeared a few seconds only—not, as would have been supposed, sinking deep down. The peculiar position of the arms and legs until the water is reached, entirely breaks the fall, and the diver is no sooner under water, than you see him clambering up again to repeat the process.

It must require considerable practice to manage the plunge as neatly as these divers, but they seem to do nothing else, and to live very comfortably on the liberal presents received. There are two of these wells, the water from one of which only is drinkable, the other being sulphurous and impure. They are said to have been built by Sultan Sham-shood-deen-Badshah, seven or eight centuries ago, at the time of the erection of the Kootub.

Adjoining is a most extensive Mahometan

cemetery, in a series of curious enclosures, in which are some very beautiful marble tombs; that of one—Fyz Mahomed Khan—is particularly noticeable in respect of the carving and fretwork around it, executed in the same material. Round about this "City of the Dead"—truly a small city—are a swarm of beggars, diseased and deformed persons, whom it is exceedingly troublesome to get rid of, and highly offensive to come in contact with. Giving only aggravates the evil, as if you give to one swarm, another appears to spring out of the tombs after you. The man in charge of the graveyard told us that there were some 600 persons living in and about the place, whose occupation was—nothing, like his own; but who seemed to be amply supported by the charity of visitors and such endowment as may have been left by the faithful buried there, the "residents" of the place having an hereditary right to the income thus derived.

The Kootub Minar now stands before you in all its massive yet elegant proportions. The buildings of which it originally formed the centre and chief ornament have decayed to a picturesque ruin, but the noble column remains untouched, apparently, by the hand of time, and bids fair to outlive many another generation.

THE KOOTUB MINAR

The tower, which is the highest column known, is built of red sandstone in five stories, narrowing gradually, from a circumference at the base of 159 feet to one at the top of 36 feet. Around each story run several horizontal belts, elaborately inscribed with passages from the Koran—very marvels of patient genius. The summit is reached by an interior winding staircase, lighted by loopholes of great breadth inside, but narrowing to almost vanishing-point as they reach the outer thickness of the wall, focussing thus, as it were, the outer light from without. A survey of the huge blocks of sandstone, hard almost as granite, with which the tower is built, with the prodigious circumference of the base, diminishes the scepticism first entertained as to the endurance of the structure through so many years. On each story is a balcony, where you gladly rest between the pauses of the ascent, which is by 375 steps of about a span each. The tower is 242 feet high to its *present* summit, the top canopy having been removed, when struck by lightning, some few years ago.* This exceedingly ornamental cupola has been

* It is said that the only Mahometan building known to be taller than this is the mosque of Hassan, at Cairo.

erected on a piece of ground adjoining, and when on the summit of the tower, must have added greatly to its effect. A reference to the drawing will show in the foreground this upper story, and on the summit of the tower will be noticed the iron railing which takes its place.

The Kootub is reputed to have been built some 700 or 800 years ago, by Sultan Sham-Shood-deen, in honour of the holy fakir who foretold him the birth of an heir; and it is stated that it took forty years to complete. The legend also runs that it was erected by the Rajah of Prithie for a favourite daughter, who desired to possess a tower with its top nigh unto heaven, from whence she might offer up her prayers.

Other accounts describe the Kootub as one of two minars designed by Sultan Sham-Shood-deen to flank a mighty mosque in everlasting remembrance of Kootub-ood-deen, who, to his qualities of general, added those of a saint. His tomb is still venerated and maintained with some show of state, being visited by thousands of devout Mussulmen. From out of the chaos of legend and superstitious chronicles it is impossible to gather any certain or precise information as to the origin of this famous structure. Probability seems to point, however, to the supposition already previously mentioned—that Sham-Shood-deen erected it, at the instigation of his general Kootub, to commemorate the victories over the Hindoos gained by the latter; and the more especially to mark the circumstance, built it in the midst of the scene of the former splendours of the vanquished Prithie Rajah.

Ascending the seemingly interminable spiral staircase, and arrived breathless at the top story, a most superb view of the surrounding country is obtained. Immediately below lie the picturesque ivy-covered ruins surrounding the tower, filled with innumerable brilliant-plumed parrots, noisily filling the air with their screams. In almost indestructible masses, scattered for miles, are seen the ruins of the old cities of Delhi, with the Jumna glistening in its snake-like silvery windings amongst the crumbling remains of the fallen greatness it survives. To the right, perched upon the summit of a range of sandstone rocks, rise, in majestic stupendousness, the frowning ruins of the fortress of Tugluckabad, erected by the Emperor Tugluck the First. The huge stones composing this, independent as they are of cement, attest the massiveness of construction of those days. Far around is a richly-cultivated plain, while the white dome of Humayoon's tomb, and the still more distant glittering minarets of the Jumna Musjid, rise far off clear against the sky. Where you stand high perched up aloft, though the sun is hotly shining, you feel quite cold, and the wind rushes round you so as to necessitate the employment of one hand in holding on your hat, while with the other you steady yourself against the breeze by the iron railing of the tower.

Sir Charles Metcalfe's house lies a short distance below. He was Resident at the Court of Delhi in the time of Akbar Shah, the father of the ex-King, and seems to have exercised to the full his fancy, first in selecting for his residence what was originally a tomb, and after, in decorating and ornamenting it from the neighbouring ruins. The custodian of the vast cemetery near the Kootub pointed to a tomb, from which the Resident, he said, had appropriated the surrounding carved marble screen.

Adjoining the Kootub are an extensive series of Hindoo ruins, originally appertaining to the palace of the Prithie Rajah. They are generally considered as by far the most interesting group of Hindoo remains that exist in India. They are believed to date as far back as the ninth century.* Built of the familiar red sandstone, they are supposed to have formed open colonnades surrounding the Prithie Rajah's palace, and are so overloaded with ornamental carving, that there is not one inch of plain surface to be seen. Figures of Hindoo gods adorn the roof and shafts of the pillars, but they are in many mutilated, doubtless by the Mahometans, who first took possession of the place.

On the eastern side of the remains, as seen to the right of the drawing, are the ruins of a beautiful range of arches, now in picturesque decay, which doubtless formed part of the before-mentioned building. A short distance to the right of the Kootub Pillar, also, is a second unfinished Minar, nearly double the dimensions of the first, and designed to eclipse that in grandeur, as it, in its turn, had eclipsed all else; but the death of its founder, and the troublous times which ensued, effectually prevented its further progress; and so it now stands in its unfinished magnificence, impressing the beholder with awe at the vastness of the mighty conception.

* The date of most of the buildings which surround the Kootub is known from the inscriptions which cover them, and they extend from 1196 to 1235.

Opposite the picturesque, wide-spanning arch, and half-fallen wall, embowered in creeping plants, as seen in the engraving, stands a curious forged iron pillar. The chief interest attaching to this is the legend which states that it "rests on the head of the serpent which supports the world, and that it marks the centre of the earth." Tradition asserts that once upon a time the Rajah of Prithie, one of the early Hindoo monarchs of Delhi, anxious to assure himself of this fact, ordered the foundations to be uncovered and the pillar upraised. This being done, blood was seen to issue from the base, and a voice heard proclaiming that for his disbelief the Rajah should cease to reign. It is to this day held, by the fanatical Hindoo, that the fall of the Rajah, some years later, was but this foretold punishment. Since then it is believed that no one has been or ever will be able to move it, and the indent of a cannon ball on its upper surface is pointed to as a living proof of its immortality. It has, however, been well ascertained by boring that the foundation of the pillar is but fourteen feet deep, but from respect to the religious prejudices of the natives it has not been deemed advisable to interfere with or to remove it. Of its real origin there is no authentic account extant, but it probably was erected in commemoration of some great victory.

It is greatly to the credit of our Government that the wondrous antiquities of the Kootub have been, by a little timely attention, preserved from sharing the fate of the ruins around. To the Marquis Dalhousie belongs the credit of their restoration. In his Minute on his Administration, addressed to the Court of Directors in 1856, he says :—

"The attention of the Government having been drawn to the fact that the noble arches and other remains of ancient architecture in the immediate vicinity of the Kootub, at Delhi, were in such disrepair, that there was danger of their falling in, and of their being thus lost to the world, immediate orders were given for their preservation.

"At the same time general instructions were issued to the officers of Government, declaring the desire of the Governor-General in Council that all such interesting and instructive monuments of former people and former days should be carefully preserved; and that the executive officers at Agra, Delhi, and wherever such remains are to be found, should consider it to be a part of their duty to see that they were upheld and sedulously cared for."

It is to be hoped that such liberal policy may be long continued, and the mighty relics of a great historical past be thus preserved to the admiration of many ages.

On the return homeward, some six miles to the south-east of Delhi, you reach another celebrated structure—Humayoon's tomb. Humayoon Shah was the first of the Moguls who was buried in India, and his tomb forms a most striking object among the sights of old Delhi. The road to it is marked on each side with crumbling ruins, graveyards with their tombs now almost disappeared, once stately mosques, now rich in vegetation, and lofty arches still bravely holding their own against the ravages of Time, but as surely yielding gradually and evidently beneath his unsparing hand.

The approach to the site of the monument is through a lofty and imposing gateway of red sandstone, inlaid with pilasters of white granite and flutes of marble; but the angles of the two sides face outwards instead of, as usual, inwards. Within the gate, a stone wall encloses a square space of about eleven acres of ground, in the centre of which stands the building. It is situated on a double platform, the lower raised four feet above the ground; from this, the second platform is ascended by a flight of twenty-six stone-steps. This upper terrace thus stands forty feet clear above the lower foundation; and in the centre of this elevated spot, which is paved with large blocks of sandstone, and measures 280 feet square, stands the tomb.

The building itself is of the usual red sandstone, most artistically picked out in relief in white marble, presenting, as viewed from a distance, the delicacy of pencil inlaying. The shape is an octagon, with all the windows recessed. The lower doors are filled in with open carved screen-work, cut out of the solid stone and marble; and above, in several parts, is seen the emblem of the Triple Tau—familiar to Royal-Arch Masons—inlaid with black marble.

There is in front a vast porch with a pointed arch, some 40 feet high, above which, surmounting the cornice at each angle, are open chamber cupolas, and small separate columnar minarets. On the reverse side of the building is a similar porch, but the actual entrance is from the side.

The centre hall under the dome is also octagonal, 43 feet in diameter and 80 feet high. It has eight approaches filled in with open carved screen-work, cut out of the solid stone, thus subduing the intensity of the glare from without, besides adding grace and lightness to the structure. The sarcophagus itself is of plain marble on a raised black and white marble platform in geometric pattern.

The floor is of marble, as are also the walls up to the height of five feet. Outside this centre hall runs a corridor, leading to four separate octagonal chambers, which contain the sarcophagi of the wife and children of the Emperor; the actual graves being, in each case, as usual, below in the vaults. In the thickness of the walls a stone staircase leads to a gallery some 40 feet high, level with the ceiling of the four smaller chambers, and looking down into the centre halls and open court; while a second staircase, rising from this level, conducts to the roof of the building, from which springs the huge dome, covered throughout its upper curve with slabs of pure white marble. The wall of the dome is 11 feet thick, and from eight openings in it, filled in with the carved screen-work before described, you look down a giddy depth into the vast hall beneath.

It was to Humayoon's tomb, after our last capture of Delhi, that the King, Bahadoor Shah—the last of the Moguls—and his sons fled and hid themselves, where they were all seized by Major Hodson—the renowned Colonel of Hodson's Horse.

Coming fresh from an inspection of the Jumna Musjid on the one side, or the Kootub Minar on the other, Humayoon's tomb does not, at first sight, impress you as it otherwise would. But the unity and beauty of the structure seem to increase as you gaze on it, and one cannot but return gratified beyond measure to have had the opportunity of viewing this masterpiece of a bygone age.

A walk of a quarter of a mile from this spot leads to a cemetery, some 500 or 600 years old, where lie the remains of Nizamooddeen Owleeah, Mahomed Shah, Mirza Jehangir, and the daughter of Shah Jehan. The carved marble screens with which these tombs are enclosed surpass in delicacy and finish even the carvings at the Taj, and are well worthy a visit.

There is also a large tank well, 49 fect square, adjoining, built in with masonry, somewhat similar to those at the Kootub. The distance down to the water's edge is 35 feet, and the depth of water 40 feet; the approach being by a broad flight of stone-steps. Whilst we were inspecting the well, a man suddenly appeared at the top of a mosque, by the edge of the tank, ran nimbly down the curve of the dome, and sprang feet foremost into the depth, rising in a few seconds with hands extended for buck-sheesh. Taking the height of the dome into account, the leap could not have been less than 100 feet, and I thought the diver well deserved the reward he received. The water of this tank is intensely cold, as from the high buildings with which it is surrounded the sun shines on it but two or three hours a day.

Sightseeing in England I have always considered the most fatiguing of pleasures, and now that we had completed an inspection of the chief celebrities of Delhi, I felt that sight-seeing in India too had its drawbacks. I don't believe that residents of Delhi are anything like so much impressed with the presence around them of these mighty relics of the past as are strangers visiting the place. It is like the Londoner who boasted, to the astonishment of his country cousins, that he had never been up the Monument or into St. Paul's. But the Delhi folk take much pride in their Public Gardens. These are situated in the centre of the town, and originally appertained to the palace, but are now called the "Queen's Gardens." Although by no means cultivated with the finish that one might expect, they form a charming retreat from the heat and dust of the city, and their many grand old trees and giant shrubs afford most grateful drives and shady evening and morning walks. The canal already referred to runs very refreshingly through the gardens, and permits of irrigation in the lower land after the Indian fashion, viz., by flooding through means of aqueducts. In one part of the grounds is a huge hollow marble basin, standing on four carved feet. It appears to be cut out of the solid block, and is 9 feet square and 4½ feet high. In the gardens, under a shed, is also a life-size model of an elephant, built of straw and covered with mud, which, at a distance, or when coming suddenly upon it, you may well mistake for the animal itself, so ingeniously is it imitated.

There is, besides, some three miles from the city, the Roshunara Bagh (so named after one of the Queens of Delhi), a vast extent of ground of many acres, covered in luxurious profusion with wood. Here is almost every known Indian tree, and the place is full of all kinds of fruit, which is farmed out by Government. These gardens formerly belonged to the ex-King, but were confiscated subsequently to the Mutiny. It is greatly to be regretted that so luxuriantly-wooded a spot should be left, as it appears to be, quite uncared for, and that which might with proper care become a delightful sylvan retreat, be allowed to degenerate into a not very health-giving jungle. The place (owing, I suppose, to the quantity of decayed vegetable matter) is infested with flies to an extent that renders walking there a task of no small discomfort; otherwise the gardens are worthy a visit.

At one end of the city is the church, at the ball and cross of which the Sepoys amused themselves by firing musketry. Since our reoccupation a new ball and cross have been erected, the mutilated ones finding a fitting resting-place, amongst other curiosities, as previously stated, in the Museum of Delhi. The city was altogether in possession and at the absolute disposal of the rebels for five months, viz., from the 11th May to the 14th September, during which time the mutineers wreaked their vengeance on everything belonging to the English within reach.

The church, which was built entirely at the cost of the celebrated Colonel Skinner (of Skinner's Horse), is supposed to be a model of St. Paul's Cathedral. But it is a very pale imitation. There are a few tombs in the churchyard: some of these have been defaced by the mutineers, and, little to the credit of our Government, they have not been restored. The large tomb in front surmounted by a marble cross marks the spot where the Beresford family, and those murdered with them during the Mutiny, lie interred; but the inscription on the tomb has become so indistinct as to be scarcely readable, although its restoration would not cost Government 10 rupees. Sir Theophilus Metcalfe is buried here; and a handsome tomb, surrounded by a beautiful railing of open carved marble, marks his grave. The two sons of Colonel Skinner also repose here under very handsome marble tombs.

Delhi is a very agreeable place of residence in the cold season, and the numbers passing through it, *en route* to the Hills, create plenty of bustle and change, and vary agreeably the monotony of Indian city life. But, strange to say, with so large an influx of visitors, there is not a decent hotel in the place, and even the Dâk Bungalow is greatly to be preferred to any of the hotels, as saving your purse and your temper, and adding to your comfort at the same time.

As to climate, a writer describing Delhi in 1835, says:—"It is considered to be one of the hottest places in India, owing probably to the arid nature of the country all around it, the immense quantity of buildings, which become so many reflectors, and the exceeding fury of the fiery simooms which blow until 10 o'clock at night, and sometimes do not subside during the twenty-four hours. This kind of weather lasts four months, and European residents must content themselves with indoor amusements for the whole period of its duration."

The rains, however, are not so disagreeable; but there is one plague from which the city and its environs are never exempt—that of flies, which come in armies similar to those which invaded Egypt in the time of Pharaoh. The time of my visit being that of the N.W. Monsoon, I did not suffer from the heat; but I can testify to this plague of flies, the like of which I never witnessed, and which in the hot season must render the place, I should think, almost unbearable.

Delhi has also a most unenviable notoriety from being afflicted with a pest called the Delhi boil, the origin and radical treatment of which has till now baffled medical skill. I have been told that it may be avoided by drinking water from the Jumna, filtered, instead of well-water.*

* A friend, long resident in Delhi, has favoured me with the following prescription, which he states is an effectual

But there are few new comers who escape it. This pest is said to be in a great measure attributable to the once crowded and dirty state of the city.

Having spent three days most agreeably in and around "Shahjehanabad the Magnificent," I now prepared for the long dâk journey before me by a careful overhaul of the provision basket, not omitting to add a bundle of wax candles, for in the dâk bungalows on the mountains the primitive "dip" alone is known, and then seldom accompanied with snuffers. It then became necessary to make arrangements for a dâk. There are here, as at most places on the Grand Trunk Road, several competitors, in the passenger transit line, for public favour, all equally notable for promises without performances in the matter of public comfort and convenience. But still the expense of the long journey from Delhi to Kalka, and back, is certainly moderate—costing (with a little bargaining) but 50 rupees.

Having heard much of the beauty of native

cure for this pest:—"Boil an ounce each of raw wax and *chumaylee* oil together, and add a sprinkling of sugar of lead. Apply this ointment twice a day, after washing the sore with tepid soap and water. In fifteen days a complete cure will be effected."

women, but never having seen any evidence of it in Calcutta, I fancied that I might be more fortunate up-country. I am fain to confess, however, that in the Punjab and North-West the women are as unattractive as in Bengal. I refer, of course, to those *seen.* Of those dark-skinned, black-eyed beauties who may be wasting their sweetness in the zenana of some Hindoo or Mussulman lord, I am content to believe all the poetical things that have been written of them; although, I fear, even these, on acquaintance, would fall far short of the ideal, as, indeed, does everything Indian.

I have heard people object often that one must not expect to find beauty amongst the country people and villagers. I cannot see why. Beauty of form or feature is not confined to rank; and I think it must be taken as somewhat conclusive evidence, therefore, that the absence of beauty among the population seen, is indicative of a want of it amongst the race generally.

There may be, and doubtless are, striking exceptions here and there; but they *are* exceptions. This, I do not think, can be said of the women of our own or any other country, where downright plainness of face and deformity of person are the exception, cheery good looks the rule, and fascinating beauty by no means rare.

I trust the reader will pardon this digression; but I think that in a book professing to instruct the uninitiated in all the sights and scenes of the route, I could not well omit to record that the majority of Eastern "beauties" whom it falls to the traveller's lot to observe are stunted damsels with ungraceful gait and expressionless countenance, clothed in a costume which, for modesty, would shock the least sensitive of European strangers of the same sex; and for dirtiness would shame St. Giles's,—an attire accompanied, nevertheless, probably by a lavish display of nose and ear rings, bangles and armlets, showing that poverty has little to do with the idiosyncrasies of the wearer.

CHAPTER IX.

DELHI TO SIMLA.

On the Grand Trunk Road—Pleasures of the Dâk Journey—Paniput—Kurnaul—Umballa—First View of the Himalayas—Tenting it—How they harness a pair—Kalka—How to cross a Mountain Stream—The Rajah of Puttiala's Gardens.

MOST travellers start from Delhi by night, to mitigate the weariness of the long dâk journey—138 miles. The plan is, however, to the timid, open to objection. The road is wholly without lights, as is also, most likely, your vehicle; for the lamps of native gharries have a most obstinate propensity for going out,—a matter not at all surprising, seeing what they are composed of. Further, the Grand Trunk Road being built in many places on very unlevel and marshy ground, frequently several feet above the land on either side, the most ready opportunity is afforded, with a careless or reckless driver and a shying horse, for a rapid somersault of yourself and vehicle. Trifling incidents of this kind, though not of every-day occurrence, are sufficiently frequent to disturb the rest of one not an old stager. I found myself on several occasions horribly aroused from a fitful sleep, to discover, when I alighted in the road, the horse and vehicle at right angles the one to the other, the driver and his mate tugging not over gently, meanwhile, at the bridle of our noble steed, and endeavouring by dint of blows, thick and fast, to persuade him of the impropriety of backing us into the ditch. But morning breaks in India very early, and you open your aching and dusty eyes to find yourself spinning along the same thin, white road, with the same flat, half-burnt-up grass-land on either side, and with the lazy cows stolidly eyeing you as you pass.

The only approach to excitement is in crossing the river channels on the route. Some of these are of great width, with their beds for the most part dry, but having, probably, in the channel some three or four feet of water. This necessitates all boxes or packages at bottom of the gharry being lifted out. These rivers are at times flooded by sudden storms, and by the melted snow from the Himalayas in the hot season, when communication is sometimes stopped for days; but, fortunately, they subside as rapidly as they rise. When approaching them, bullocks are harnessed to the gharry, and it requires sometimes two or three pairs to draw the vehicle through the fearfully uneven and soft yielding sand of the river's bed. A "spill," though not of very frequent occurrence, is sufficiently probable to induce a sharp precautionary look-out being kept. Here, again, the traveller will be applied to for bucksheesh by the gooruwallahs (bullock drivers) and coolies, which, if prudent, he will refuse. Why, up to this day, bridges have not been constructed, I am at a loss to conceive. One is in course of building at the Marcanda river, but does not appear as if it would be finished for several years to come.

Along the route you have a complete opportunity of seeing the "oppressed" ryot, who does not look so miserable under the circumstances as the good people at home are too ready to believe. That his condition is poor is greatly owing to his inherent laziness—a labouring native, agricultural or otherwise, acting on the principle, that what his father was he will be, and that if half a day's work will secure him a sufficiency of creature comforts, it is folly to labour for more. Many of the settled agriculturists themselves own plots of land, which are made to produce only so much as is absolutely necessary for subsistence, under a system of culture coeval with that of Adam. Even when improvements are placed before them, they steadily refuse to adopt them; and this is one reason why India remains so insensible to the civilizing effects of our rule. The system of periodical Agricultural Exhibitions has done some good; but the enlightenment has not as yet proceeded far into the interior.

Before reaching Kurnaul, about 54 miles from Delhi, you pass Paniput, a fortified, walled town, the sight of which reminds one of the Middle Ages, and of the walled towns of Syria. There is little specially interesting to relate of Kurnaul; it has the reputation, however, of being filthy even for a native town.* Up to the year 1838, Kurnaul was one of our frontier posts, and in 1739 an important battle was fought here between Nadir Shah, at the head of an enormous force, and Mahomed Shah, in which the latter was utterly routed.

* If the traveller desire to put up at Kurnaul, there is both a dâk bungalow and an "hotel" there, facing each other, one mile out of the town on the Grand Trunk Road. The hotel is more comfortable than the bungalow, but a little more expensive. I put up at the latter, and received every possible attention. It was then kept by one Hossein Khan, by whose name it will doubtless for many years to come be known.

Some miles before reaching Umballa, the Himalayas are seen on the right, towering aloft dimly in the distance, and in February and March snow is discernible in the crevices of the mountains.

Arrived at Umballa, thoroughly tired out, I found to my chagrin both hotel and dâk bungalow full, for during the winter, at Simla, the residents and tradesmen of the hills who do not return to Calcutta, make Umballa a temporary abode. Contrary to the rule, and most unfairly, one family had been occupying the bungalow for several days; but I was informed that, if I went to some official, half a dozen miles distant, he would *possibly* interfere in my behalf. This was buying comfort at almost too high a price; so I elected rather to appeal to the sympathies of the landlord of the hotel, who agreed to rig me up a small tent in the compound. Tent-living, I have been told, is very jolly—when you're used to it. I dare say it is. Probably it was owing to the fact of my not being used to it, that it struck me as the reverse of jolly. However, it answered the purpose, and was a great deal preferable to another night in the dâk gharry. I can, at any rate, speak well of the hotel. I have never seen in India such well-ordered, nor such thoroughly respectful and attentive servants; everything about the place bore the aspect of constant supervision. The charges also were very moderate (4 rupees per diem). If time be not an object, a stay of a night here breaks the journey most pleasantly.

Umballa is important as being a principal military station, the head-quarters of a division of the army. Its European population is, however, of a very migratory character; for in the hot season, all who can, desert it for the hills.

Your body, if not your mind, rested by the brief stoppage here, you bundle bag and baggage into the dâk carriage once more, and set off again *en route* for the hills. Up to Umballa only one horse is put to your dâk gharry, but you are now permitted the luxury of a pair, owing to the steep and heavy nature of the road from hence to Kalka. The method of harnessing adopted is very original. In place of the usual splinter bar and pole, the shafts are allowed to remain in, one side of them being made to do duty for a pole. A bamboo is then lashed with rope to the shaft, projecting several feet necessarily on *one side* of the gharry, and to this the second horse is attached. So that instead of the strength of the horses being directed to the centre of the gharry, that of one is, as it were, pulling away from it, more especially so when one or other of the poor quadrupeds takes it into his head to perform a *pas seul.* The springs of the dâk gharries are, on account of the roughness of the hill road, "packed" with bamboo, and well enwrapped in rope. From the actual necessity for this, as Kalka is approached, some idea may be gathered of the jolting the unfortunate traveller is subjected to.

Encouraged probably by companionship, your steeds seem now to take to the collar with better heart, and along you spin at a headlong pace down one hill and up another, in a very alarming way, the gharry rocking about in a manner suggestive of "a spill"—a possibility rendered nearer by the sight of an overturned vehicle in the ditch by the roadside, which nobody seems to have thought it worth while to pick up; for you see it as you return, and, for aught I know, it may be there now.

There is now no mistake about your proximity to the Himalayas. What a few hours ago loomed out indistinct against the horizon, now stands sharply defined in lofty heights, uprising one above another, and affording to the eye, accustomed for many years to the dead level plains, a surprising and gratifying novelty. Crossing the stony causeway of a mountain stream, and mounting with difficulty a series of low brushwood-clothed hills, you come in sight of the village of Kalka, the starting point for the journey across the mountains. Kalka is a curious and exceedingly ugly little mud and stone village, perched on the lower spurs of the Himalayas, and from the heights above a keen fresh air is nearly always blowing, even in the very hottest weather. Although I had been by no means frozen in travelling to this point, here I found it uncomfortably cold, and was not sorry to see, in one of the funny little hotels of this funny little place, a cheerful-looking fire.

I don't think I ever parted with anything with less regret than I now did with my dâk gharry, which was, on my evacuating it, hauled up with ropes by coolies, to do duty presently for some unfortunate voyager to the plains, whom I really began quite to compassionate; and I almost forgot my own recent sufferings in contrasting the exhilarating journey upon which I was about to embark, with the wearisome one I had just performed.

While arrangements were being made for a conveyance to the Hills, I paid a hurried visit to some very curious gardens, four miles below Kalka, belonging to the Rajah of Puttiala. They are formed in a series of natural terraces, and have basins and fountains of water running through, from the highest to the lowest terrace, the effect of which, when the water is in full play, must be most charming. The ground comprises in extent about 150 acres; and the produce is farmed out to a native gardener for 1,200 rupees a year. I asked this man how much it yielded him yearly, and he admitted a profit of 3,000 rupees; but it yields probably double that. It is crowded with fruit-trees of every conceivable kind, and has no less than 2,000 orange trees, which, at the time of our visit, were full of fruit, and presented a most novel and refreshing appearance.

There are several summer-house looking buildings about the grounds, which European gentlemen are allowed to occupy for a few days, by application to the manager of the Rajah's affairs. The place might, with a large expenditure, be rendered exquisitely beautiful and ornamental, since it possesses great natural advantages; but, beyond attention to the cultivation of the fruit-trees, it seems to receive no care. The malee who farms the produce, and who jealously and suspiciously follows you over the place, is not above asking or expecting a douceur.

CHAPTER X.

SIMLA AND THE SNOWY RANGE.

Methods of crossing the Hills—The Jhampan—The Old and New Route—"Over the Hills and far away"—Hill Men—Mountain Scenery—Military Stations—Simla—The Seasons, and the "Season"—Specialities of Simla—Rents and Methods of Furnishing—Market Prices—Servants—Means of Locomotion—Places of Interest—Climate, &c.—The Snowy Range.

TO the sun-dried traveller from the plains, the atmosphere, even at the slight elevation of the first range of hills on which Kalka is situate, is wonderfully invigorating. The air blows refreshingly down from the mountains, which commence here to tower abruptly upward, their summits hidden, perchance, in fleecy clouds of mist, or dwarfed by still higher ascending peaks beyond; while ever and anon, as the sun illumines their sides, or the shadow of a dark cloud reflects its gloom upon them, a powerful contrast is produced on the mind just fresh from a contemplation of the interminable dreary level of the plain seen lying like a mirage far away in the distance below.

The mode of transit to the Hills is by jhampans, or by ponies, and all luggage is, by the old road, carried up by coolies. The jhampan is a kind of sedan-chair, closed on its four sides only by curtains—once red—and lined to match. It is carried on the shoulders of four men by a pole front and rear. So long as you are on level ground, the position is not very different from that in an ordinary palkee, except that, being lighter, the contrivance has much more swing; but seeing that you are always either going up or down steep inclines, your head is necessarily in a most uncomfortable position of restraint, and a couple of hours' experience of jhampan riding sufficed to give me a splitting headache. Ladies, nevertheless, mostly choose this mode of conveyance. You can, however, go on horseback; and to one accustomed to the saddle, and not nervous about precipices, that is by far the most comfortable method. But it is very needful before starting to lift the saddle, and see if there be a sore on the animal's back, as out of three ponies taken by our party, two were from this cause unfit for use; and the contingency in such case of your steed pitching you down a khud some thousand feet or more is thus by no means remote.

The hire of a jhampan is 3 rupees the journey,

and the pay of each man 1 rupee. The hotel-keeper charges also a commission of 6 pice per man. Eight men are the complement of each jhampan, four to carry and four as relays; and if, with the luggage coolies, the number engaged amounts to twenty-five men, it is, strange to say, compulsory to engage also a *mate*, though his duties extend no further than affording a sort of nominal security for the coolies' good behaviour. For this service the mate mulcts you of 1-12 rupees the journey. These rates apply to what is termed the old road: for there are two routes to Simla; the charge per man by the new road being 6 annas higher. This new road has been constructed to facilitate the conveyance of goods to the Hills. It is a comparatively broad path, protected in great part by fencing and stonework; and although it has cost a prodigious sum per mile, the entire road having had to be blasted from the solid rock, or carried over mountain streams by bridges, it is in point of convenience worth the money. Perhaps for picturesqueness the old road is the best, but for comfort the new one is vastly superior; and, although thirteen miles longer, I am sure that you more than save the distance by the extra speed at which you can travel. If on horseback, you may go at a hand-gallop almost all the way; while by the old way you are no sooner up one steep incline than you have to go down another, until, on arriving within three miles of Simla itself, there is a hill almost perpendicular—enough to break the wind of man or beast to climb.

The origin of the construction of this new road is thus explained :—

"The work had its origin in the desire entertained by the Government to abolish, and to remove all pretext for defending, Begaree (or the system of employing the forced labour of coolies) in the hills. So far as the Government was concerned, that system had the sanction of treaties; for every chief was bound, whenever he should be called upon, to find upon his own part bands of labourers for the temporary service of the State.

"The Government has always amply remunerated the coolies, who were so employed, for the time they served. But the money was usually in great measure taken from them by their own chiefs on their return. They were forced to travel great distances; and in many ways they suffered oppression from the duty.

"The abuse of the system by private individuals was believed to be great, though every endeavour upon the part of the Government was steadily made to check it.

"Yet the evil of the system itself was unavoidable by any means. So long as the hill roads, even to the English settlements and military stations, continued to be little better than mountain paths, no other labour than that of men could transport whatever was to be carried, and no substitute for Begaree could be found. The first step, therefore, and the only step, necessary for the abolition of Begaree, was to construct a system of roads which would admit of all articles being carried upon beasts of burden, or even dragged in wheeled conveyances of various kinds.

"For the furtherance of this purpose, a road, first designed by Major Kennedy and executed by Lieutenant Briggs, has been constructed from the plains at Kalka to the hill-station of Simla. It is about fifty miles in length, already sixteen feet in breadth, and it has nowhere a steeper gradient than three feet in the hundred, constituting a hardly perceptible rise.

"From this road branches have been carried to the military stations at Kussowlee and

Subathoo; and a branch is now being made to connect those stations with the plains towards the Sutlej." *

Going up, our party consisted of three, and all of us being fond of exercise, we found it both agreeable and economical so to arrange that we should take it in turns to walk. After the heat of the Plains, the cool bracing atmosphere of the Mountains is most invigorating, and one feels at first inclined to tramp along for miles. Walking, however, like most other things, requires practice, especially along a hill-path of not the smoothest description; and I found a four-mile stretch quite sufficient to tire me thoroughly, and make me glad to change about with my companion who had the pony.

The great extent to which the hills are cultivated, is the first noticeable peculiarity. Looking at the lofty masses of stone around you, with only the scantiest of gorse-grass occasionally clothing their stony sides, one hardly expects to find much arable land, for even in the valleys there is scarcely a quarter of an acre approaching to level ground. A most ingenious and painstaking plan, however, has been adopted, of forming the slopes of the

* Marquis Dalhousie's Minute to the Court of Directors, 1856.

hills, where at all practicable, into terraces, and there making a soil. Some of these terraces are so narrow that a plough could hardly be run along them, yet there they exist in thousands at one part and another, looking fresh with their soil newly turned, or green with the early corn. The territory appertains to the Rajah of Puttiala (whose predecessor acted well during the Mutiny), and he farms out these plots of ground to the hill men at an almost nominal rental. These hill dwellers are a much fairer and more powerful race than is seen in the plains, but barbaric to a degree in their habits and dress. They wear loose pointed slippers on the feet, wrap themselves thickly round with a large *resai*,* swathing up their heads and faces like so many mummies, and the women and children wear pantaloons of blue cotton, fitting tightly to the skin. They are all repulsively filthy in their habits—more so, if possible, than the natives in the plains, and appear never to wash. A more thoroughly useless-looking individual than one of these men working, on a cold day, at the roads, swathed up to the eyes, and with only his hands visible, can hardly be imagined.

The old road up the mountain averages 10

* A quilt made of cotton wool, and lined.

feet wide, winding round and round successive perpendicular heights. Frequently there are very dangerous - looking curves, where it seemingly only requires a strong puff of wind to tilt you over the side. Occasionally you meet a troop of bullocks or donkeys, and it would be by no means pleasant to have at such a *rencontre* a skittish horse. On the old road there is no protection against such an accident as might thus arise; but on the new one, for the greater part of the way, there is a strong parapet wall, or else boundary posts.

The scenery along the route, though somewhat uniform and monotonous, is in parts grand and imposing. Huge rocky hills rise abruptly to a height of from 500 to 1,000 feet, or undulate along to a much steeper ascent in the distance; while towards the valleys shine out the bright green patches of cultivation on the hill-side terraces, down which, noisily making their way through many a rocky ravine, rush bright sparkling waterfalls, tumbling and leaping in frothy beauty as they are checked in their course to the channels below, where massive boulders of stone lie mingled with the rounded pebbles, once as giant-like as themselves. And then there are the masses of wild honey-suckle, the eccentric cactus, and the creeping vine running over and clothing the rugged points of rock; and the feathery bamboo, its delicate foliage trembling in the wind, and contrasting fancifully with the lofty pine towering nobly by its side. As the sun bursts out from behind a cloud, the mountains change their hue, and what seemed only a dark and frowning rocky height before, is changed to a smiling green-clad slope; while the hills in shadow behind, yet half tinged with the reflected light, become blue, rich brown, or purple, as the ever-varying shadow of the cloud interrupts or in part reveals the glorious sun. Occasionally a troop of wild monkeys will rush chattering up the cliff, pelting you from the top with pebbles, —separating in their ascent the loose shingly soil, which comes rattling in a shower down the hill-side, and speeds headlong away to the valley beneath. Here the eagle is also seen, swooping grandly over some lofty mountain peak; while the ignoble carrion kite hovers, screaming, about the valleys. Again, as dusk draws near, light fleecy clouds shroud the tops of neighbouring hills in mist; and still, winding your way toilsomely up the height, you see below you these same nuclei of vapour floating uncertainly in mid air. The majesty of effect, however, which would be caused by the great height of the mountain-tops from the plains if seen at once, is lost to a great extent by reason of hill rising on hill in such succession, that, as you ascend, what one hour is the crest of a mountain, the next appears as but a part of the valley beneath.

Along the range you pass other sanitaria besides Simla. Thus, on the old road we have Kussowlie; whilst on the new there is Dugshai and Subathoo.* Kussowlie, though actually higher than Simla, is by no means so cold, being further removed from the Snowy Range. The white-capped tops of many a mountain are, however, to be seen during several months of the year; and there is generally snow in the higher ravines near and adjoining the Snowy Range, of which a good view is here obtained.

On our road up we were nigh being weather-bound on the mountains, a violent storm from the upper hills overtaking us; but we were fortunately near to the Saree Bungalow, and so obtained shelter for the night; and, sitting

* All military stations. At Kussowlie is the Lawrence Asylum—an admirable institution now under the control of Government, for the education and care of soldiers' or officers' children left destitute.

by our not very brilliant fire, we thanked our stars we were not on the slippery mountain path. The wind rushed sweeping down from the lofty ranges above, whistled and roared through the valley, and hurled the misty vapour so thickly over all, as to render the atmosphere impalpable for hours; while the rain fell in a torrent of biting, whirling sleet, frightening the cattle to shelter. The following morning all trace of the downpour, beyond a few puddles, had disappeared; but the wind still continued dangerously strong, as we struggled against it along the narrow path; and on arriving at Simla, several hours behind time, we found a severe snow-storm had fallen, leaving its traces in several inches of crisp snow.

I should mention that we journeyed up by the old road, and came down by the new one; and for the information of those who might choose to do the same, and, indeed, for those going by either route, I append a list of the respective dâk bungalows, and their distances apart:—

Old Road.		New Road.	
From	*Miles.*	*From*	*Miles.*
Kalka to		Kalka to	
Kussowlie	9	Dhurrumpore	15
Hurreepore	15	Solun	11
Syree	10	Kearee	$14\frac{1}{2}$
Simla	9	Simla	$15\frac{1}{2}$
Total	43	Total	56

The dâk bungalows, both here and on the Grand Trunk Road, though undoubted conveniences, are about as uncomfortable and wretched in appearance and fittings as can be imagined. An old sinner, in the shape of a khansamah, is the genius of the place, and has rarely aught else to tempt the tired traveller with than a "sudden death"—a fowl caught running in the yard, and dished up forthwith; though, occasionally, in the hill bungalows you do get some good mutton.

There is, be it remembered, nothing in the way of sleeping accommodation at the bungalows but a charpoy, and here you again especially need your resai, pillows, and railway rug. Indeed, the sensation of feeling thoroughly cold was quite a luxury, and I gave myself up in real ecstasy to violent pantomimic attempts at circulating the blood. A draught of the mountain air, too, in the early morning, acted as a powerful tonic, and I found myself complacently devouring the toughest of viands with almost good temper.

As we were in no hurry, and wished to fully enjoy the mountain scenery, we proceeded very leisurely on our journey, which occupied in all three days,* much to the gratification of our

* It is quite practicable, by laying a pony dâk a full day

jhampan wallahs, who trudged bravely along, chanting a wild, monotonous kind of dirge. One generally droned the air, and the others chanted the refrain. The jhampan wallahs have a most peculiar shuffling gait, caused probably by wearing slippers considerably too large for them. Much of your comfort depends upon the sort of bearers you get, as some keep step very imperfectly, and the result is that you feel the motion in every bone of your body. But where the bearers carry you with an even sling trot, you soon get accustomed and indifferent to the motion, if the ground is only at all level.

In some parts of the road it is all but impracticable to do other than get out and walk; and, as I said before, the immediate approach to Simla is a fearful piece of climbing. It was snowing hard when we reached the summit of the ascent, and we found ourselves surrounded everywhere by pure white drift—extremely

before, to reach Simla in one day. The hotel-keeper will arrange this, if need be, for you, by sending on word to the bungalows to have a pony in readiness at each. Ponies can mostly be got on hire at the dâk bungalows *without* notice; but, of course, there is no certainty in this, and the former is the only safe plan. The hire of a pony is eleven rupees by either road; but out of the season they may be had for less.

pretty to look at, but uncommonly unpleasant to have to face. No troops of smart equestrians or vigorous-looking foot passengers were to be seen, as "in the season." Now and then a native, shrouded in a blanket, shrunk grudgingly along; or a packhorse, laden with wood, obstructed the path. All looked as bleak and forbidding as could well be, and the atmosphere breathed nothing but flakes of snow. However, on we toiled, and after nigh an hour's tussle against the storm, along the slippery narrow winding path, we reached Rujeeb Ali's caravanserai, where we were conducted to a cavernous sort of apartment, boasting certainly a fireplace, but innocent evidently of the presence of a fire for long past. Mine host looked at us strangely, although not unwelcomely, wondering, doubtless, what on earth had induced us to visit Simla at such a time. He suggested that perhaps we should like a fire, and said, if he could find any wood that was not covered by snow, we should have one. Poor man, he did his best; but I shall long remember the chilly hours we passed in that desolate chamber, cheered by the light of but one candle —and *that* occasionally blown out by the wind; and warmed only by the dense smoke which issued from the soaked pine-logs hissing on our fire. Fortunately we had some tins of preserved soup, and, by the aid of a spirit-lamp, succeeded in heating these, and so making a rough-and-ready supper, glad, after that and a tumbler of hot grog, to creep between the blankets, which seemed now to have but little warmth left in them.

Soon after sunrise we awoke, to find the glorious sun lighting up all around, and reflecting itself dazzlingly on the snowy landscape. Borrowing a stout pronged staff, and wrapping ourselves up to the eyes, out we trudged through the deep snow, shivering at the task; but half an hour's walking, or rather wading, soon made us glad to unbutton our coats, and we returned in the jolliest of moods and the best of appetites, pleasantly excited withal by the jaunt, having narrowly escaped twice tumbling over the path to a depth of some sixty feet—once by slipping, and once from the fence giving way.

For many days we bravely faced all weathers, trudged up and down, and saw and heard all there was to be heard or seen; but our excitement and enterprise were limited necessarily to what was incidental to going up break-neck places along paths glossy with ice, along with the charm of novelty of scene, so utterly in contrast to the never-varying plains. Any place more undesirable for a residence in winter, so far as comfort is concerned, I cannot imagine. And yet to see Simla in the winter time—its fanciful summer-house dwellings covered with creamy roofs of snow; the tall pines and firs fretted over with icicles, and frosted with snow-drift on leaf and branch; the lofty mountains around all white with their fleecy canopies; the valleys clothed with winter's thick smooth carpet; and above all, to see the everlasting Snowy Range shining out in its grandest aspect, impressing the beholder with awe at its majesty and immensity—it is indeed worth while for once to essay a winter journey to the Himalayas.

A friend of mine, to whom I am indebted for much reliable information about the place, and who has had good opportunities of seeing Simla in its calmer as well as its sterner aspect, lays much stress on the advantages in point of health to be derived from a residence at this sanitarium during the winter months. He says that in summer, persons who have suffered from climatic diseases in the plains receive only a negative advantage from the hill climate.

This opinion is shared by a writer in 1831, who maintains that "two-thirds of the invalids who visit the Alpine regions for reparation of broken health merely thrive by the absence of morbid causes (viz., heat), and continue well so long as they breathe the cool air, but derive no excitation of constitution tending to permanent benefit, and are surprised to find their complaints return with the first encroachment of sultry weather—disappointed with the hills, but, in fact, only deceived by themselves."

There seems logic in the reasoning, and I am disposed to concur in the opinion that, "No radical change is effected by the hill climate, during the hot months, in cases of a disorganization of morbid functions; unless, indeed, the patient proceeds to the vicinage of the summer limit of snow, when he will, in all probability, gain sufficient stamina to resist the predisposition to tropical diseases."

In the season Simla is the gayest of places—balls, picnics, archery, amateur theatricals, and professional concerts following each other in quick succession; for Simla possesses an Assembly Room (serving also the purpose of a Theatre), a Racquet Court, and a Masonic Lodge. Besides all these, there are the Simla Volunteers, a Public Library, and a Bank, where, however, they charge you 1 *per cent.* on

Calcutta drafts! There was, and possibly still exists, a newspaper, which, like its patrons, appears there only in "the season."

The months of March and April in Simla are generally very stormy, heavy showers of rain prevailing, often accompanied by hail, rendering the weather chilly. The hailstones are all of a large size, and fall thickly, soon whitening the ground. In May and June the weather is mostly dry, and the thermometer rises in the shade sometimes so high as 84 degrees—at all times, even in winter, the rays of the sun, in clear weather, being ardent. July and August and the greater part of September are exceedingly moist and cloudy. The weather, it must be confessed, however, then becomes very gloomy; but it has been remarked that it is at this very season that gaieties of all kinds reach their climax. My good-natured "Simla Correspondent," referring to Simla at this time of the year, writes: "The hills are then usually enveloped in clouds and mist, and there is a constant pattering of rain-drops on the trees and the wooden pent-roofs. During the glimpses of bright weather, however, the clouds compensate for their previous depressing effects by presenting the eye with an endless variety of fantastic combinations, and rich colours woven in them by the beams of the sun. I have seen the whole sky filled with huge masses of clouds, except towards the west, where, under what looked like a rugged bank, there appeared, first, the smooth blue sky, like a peaceful lake, with a few purple patches of clouds for islets; then, a scarcely perceptible line of delicate green, succeeded by a line of equally delicate yellow, and then a broad belt of orange-red light. The clouds may often be seen hanging on the brow of some hill, curled up into fleecy bundles, the upper parts tinged with amber. One of the most common sights is a heavy volume of mist coming down from the top of Mount Jacko, and gradually spreading itself over the place; while the green slopes and the chimney-crested cottages melt away like a dissolving view, and are at last completely hidden from the sight, leaving the beholder to fancy himself in the midst of unbounded space, and to hear, perhaps, the hoarse croaking of some solitary raven rising from the abyss. This state of things may continue for a whole day; but it sometimes happens that the mist is suddenly drawn aside, like a curtain, and nature smiles again."

The houses at Simla are mostly built of wood with shingle roofs, slate being only used occasionally. The buildings are perched in all sorts of funny places:—here on the top of a hill, now on its slope, then deep in some valley; and the oddest roads possible lead to them, climbing, twisting, and turning round rocks, here and there built up artificially—now a ravine bridged over, and again the path level with the chimney top of some dwelling, while the entrance-door is perhaps in the roof itself. Truly one must have good lungs and stout legs to tramp up and down the declivities; but I suppose people get used to it, and the exercise at any rate seemed healthy, for everybody had the rosiest of complexions, and the cheeks of the young ladies absolutely invited kisses. A long pole, tipped at the end with iron, seemed to be a favourite and rather a useful kind of walking-stick.

Since the Government has been transferred to Simla in the summer months, rents have risen fearfully; and with the run of the fashionable world and its train to these breezy hills, all things else have proportionately increased in price. Houses which formerly let for 600 rupees the season, are now readily fetching 1,200; and there is a growing demand for accommodation. Places let out in this manner are furnished (in not too luxurious a style) by the proprietor with such articles as tables, sofas, chairs, beds, toilet-glasses, chiffoniers, fire-irons, and floor-cloths; and the tenant has only to provide himself with cooking utensils, crockery ware, and lamps. These, too, need not be purchased, for they can be hired for the season at one of the shops kept by natives in the upper bazaar. The place abounds in shops, where everything can be procured, just as in Calcutta, but *not*, however, at Calcutta rates.

Some adventurous persons convey the bulk of their household requisites from Calcutta; but I am afraid the per-centage of goods arriving in serviceable order must be small indeed, not to speak of the delay. Never were articles perishable condemned to such perils by land. Jolted out of knowledge in the railway, left on the platforms in all sorts of weather an indefinite period, in the charge of nobody in particular; pitch-forked on to rickety bullock hackeries, to be shaken as only hackeries can shake goods; lastly, to be toilsomely conveyed, probably by hand, up 7,000 or 8,000 feet of ascent, for the most part along a mountain path, edged by sheer depths of most uncomfortable profundity,—it is no wonder that people prefer paying a somewhat usurious rate of hire to incurring the risk of transit.

I witnessed on my homeward journey, however, the baggage of his Excellency the Governor-General and Staff being conveyed to the Hills for the season. An alarming train it certainly was, and no scruples as to limit, such as might be supposed to occur to ordinary mortals, seemed to have restricted the arrangements of the viceregal conveyance department.

The hill coolies, who do so much of the work of conveying luggage to Simla, are a very strong, but ugly, race of men. They do not overburden themselves with clothes, but seem to have faith in such as they wear being kept thoroughly dirty, probably with a view to "keep out the cold." They particularly affect, like the jhampan wallahs, loose—I might say dirty—slippers, in which they shuffle along the narrow, giddy, winding mountain paths at a good sling trot, with a load on their heads, or on the shoulders of two of them, such as would astonish the nerves of even a dock porter.

Visitors to Simla, unless they prefer hotel accommodation, should take early steps to secure a house, especially if they desire any particular situation. There are some who would rather avoid a northerly position, and others who object to being low down in the *Khud*, or at the extremities of Simla, at a distance from the church, the market, the theatre, the bank, the "kutcherry," and many places of business.

Formerly the "Club" used to provide almost sufficient accommodation for chance visitors; but, following the "limited" mania, this has been purchased, added to, and converted into a large hotel. There is also the hotel at which I stayed, on the top of the hill, nearly as high as Mount Jacko: a rambling sort of place, full of whirlwinds and draughts, but nevertheless commanding a good view. It is worth something, however, to go up and down the hill road leading to the place, and I should not recommend it to people with delicate lungs. A third hotel, the "Royal," is situated on the Mall.

Immediately on one's arrival in Simla, an individual of the *bunneeah* profession waits upon you, with an offer to supply, on credit, *ad libitum*, everything required, from a tea-kettle, a saucepan, or an earthen pipkin, to a maund of rice or gram. At first, until you have fairly settled down in your domicile, it is convenient to employ him; but it should only be on the distinct understanding that he must produce a receipt or voucher for everything entered in his accounts, otherwise there will most certainly be collusion between him and your servants.

The latter class, I may remark, even in the Presidency towns, far exceed, in power and practice of annoyance, Mayhew's "Greatest Plague"; but in the hills, whither he has with difficulty been seduced by offer of high wages and warm clothing, your servant becomes truly your master, and is ever ready, and it may be said ever able, to fleece you to his heart's content.

Rents, I have already stated, are very high in Simla; and the following tariff of charges (not published under authority, though) for the more important articles of consumption will give people in England an idea of the cost of edibles in the Himalayas:—

Beef—from 2rs. to 3rs. for a sirloin.

Mutton—from 12 annas to 1r. 8a., a quarter.

Fowls—from 5rs. to 8rs. for 20.

Ducks—from 9rs. to 10rs. for 20.

Eggs—4 pice each; or 25 for the rupee, if supplied regularly by a man at your house.

Rice—good, 6½ seers per rupee, and inferior 8 seers.

Bread—from 12 to 14 loaves per rupee.

Butter—from 14 to 16 chittacks per rupee.
Milk—from 16 to 18 seers ,,
Ghee—2 seers ,,
Sugar—good, 3 seers* ,,
Fruit abounds, and is cheap.

The only means of locomotion in Simla, besides that of walking, is by horses, or by jhampans—a conveyance previously described. Viewed in any way, these contrivances are scarcely *luxuries*; and, indeed, it is difficult for ladies or families to get along without them, since Aquarius is not an unfrequent visitor at Simla; and when he *does* come, it is to some purpose.

If a visitor is unwilling to incur the responsibility of keeping his "carriage-and-four," there is the almost sufficient alternative of any number of the like conveyances "on hire." But, as Jeames would say, the "kerrect" thing is to keep your jhampan.

If a jhampan is kept, the four jhampanees, or bearers, who are paid at the rate of 4-8 rupees each a month, furnish you with fuel on your providing them with axes and ropes, and paying 8 annas a month to the hill-chief from whose

* A seer is equivalent to about two pounds, and a chittack is the sixteenth part of a seer.

forests the wood is cut. They are also expected to attend to the garden, which is pretty certain to be a "hanging one." When employed on their legitimate duties, they are dressed in a motley suit of woollen, consisting of coats, caps, and trousers. A "mate," or head jhampanee, has generally to be kept, and is employed chiefly in looking after children, carrying letters, or walking by the side of the jhampan.

A timely provision of fuel is always necessary for the rainy season: the root of the oak, known to the natives by the name of *bân*, is best suited for the fireplace in the sitting or dining-room. Pine wood is consumed very rapidly, and gives but little warmth.

The Himalayas are believed to be rich in minerals; but circumstances have not as yet favoured a practical search for them. Coal exists; but in the hill-stations coals are but little used, wood being the chief article employed for fires.

The water-supply of Simla is derived from a reservoir, situated between the gorge of two hills. A prettily-constructed building covers this place, which one might suppose from its appearance to be a swimming bath. Simla possesses also a brewery and a rum and whisky distillery, the former belonging to a joint-stock company. But as elsewhere in India, beer is the great beverage. Considerable attention has been wisely bestowed of late years to the subject of the manufacture of beer in the Hills; and the experiments made have been attended with such success that Breweries have been established at Murree, Kussowlie, and Simla, supplying a remarkably good beverage, preferred, it is said, by the troops to English beer. It requires one to get used to it, however; and at first I flew from it to Bass, though ultimately I almost grew to like the former. The difference in cost is necessarily a very important element in the question; for whereas London bottled beer sells at from seven to ten rupees a dozen, the hill beer can be supplied at five rupees.

There are some pleasant spots for pic-nics, low down the mountain side, and some noted falls. The road to the waterfalls (known to the natives by the name of "Lall Panee"—Red Waters) is in many parts steep and rugged, and winds through a wilderness of cheel pines. The first fall thunders down from a height of some 50 feet. The water, gliding away from its base, soon meets with numerous obstructions, and consequently adds to the din by chafing and foaming, and forming little cascades throughout its course. At the third fall a beautiful iris is created by the sun's rays striking on the spray; and if a bright day towards the breaking-up of the rains is chosen as the time for a visit, the specialities of the falls will be seen to great advantage. Excursions are also made to a place six miles from Simla, called Mashobra, where a bungalow may be rented for the day or the month from the proprietor. Mahasoo, ten miles from Simla, where there is a dâk bungalow, the khansamah of which can serve up a good dinner, is also favoured by those desiring a change of air. Away, too, in the far Himalayas, north of Missourie, are the rapids of the mighty Ganges, which takes its rise above, in the snow-clad mountains, and whose waters, swollen by the melted snows of the lower valleys, are about this spot deemed peculiarly sacred by the Hindoos. Here is the famous temple of Gangoutrie, one of the most sacred of spots to the Brahmin.

In Simla itself, a visit should not be omitted to the top of Mount Jacko, a height from the level of the church of about 400 feet, whence, on a clear day, a good view may be obtained. The road round Jacko, a distance of about $5\frac{1}{4}$ miles, affords a charming ride, and to good

SIMLA

pedestrians a pleasant walk. It is in many parts very solitary, and overshadowed by the ilex, the rhododendron, and the keloo pine; and during the rains the hill sides are enamelled with wild geraniums, hill anemones, columbines, pheasants' eyes, and other wild flowers, which peep out from among ferns and feathery mosses.

My illustration, facing this page, is taken from the heights above the church, and gives some idea of the romantic position of the dwellings, dotted about on crags or half buried in the redundant foliage; but from the limited size of the picture, the grandeur of effect of the sudden descent to the valley is quite lost. The view from almost any part of the Hills is replete with interest and variety; but the grand vista of the Snowy Range can only be seen to perfection from few points. The frontispiece is from a drawing made on the spot, in the balcony at Rujeeb Ali's Hotel, on Jacko. The line of mountains in the distance rise to 15,000 feet high, beyond which stretches to unseen heights the everlasting snow.

These lofty ranges of mountains in the far distance, covered with eternal ice; rendered radiantly brilliant or frowningly gloomy, as the bright sun appears, or is shadowed by the frequent uprising mists from the valleys; the stately pines and the many-tinted evergreens, as seen shining in joyous radiance after a sunny shower, or framed in icy pattern by the pure white, fleecy snow; the bracing air, and the toilsome but romantic steeps, the harsh rugged hill sides and the green deep valleys—all these afford a charm, which the Himalayas perhaps alone, by such powerful and sudden contrast, present, and which thus render the Hills so grateful a retreat from the hot and monotonous existence of the plains.

But, alas! even Simla has its cemetery, and it is by no means empty. It lies very low down the Khud, and is a romantic spot. Some of the graves are overspread with clover, and others with the passion-flower. A few of the inscriptions tell of untimely deaths, by falls down a precipice in the interior. One of those who met with such an end was the late Henry Lawrence, nephew of the present Viceroy, and son of the political officer and soldier whose name, in connection with the defence of Lucknow, has become so familiar to Englishmen.

That Simla will ever be a sanitarium accessible to the multitude, is out of the question, even should the railway run close to the foot of the Hills, as is probable; but it affords a delightful change for those who have the time and money to enjoy themselves.

And now, good reader, if you have journeyed with me thus far, and are snugly ensconced in cool Simla itself, let me wish you rosy health, and as much pleasure and comfort as you can desire. Or if you have, as "gentlemen of England," stayed at home at ease, let me advise you that there is something to be said even for the perils and labour of a journey to the Snowy Range.

APPENDIX.

TABLE—*Showing the Stations from Howrah to Delhi, the distance from each, time in transit, and the* 1st *Class Railway Fares.*

Name of Station.	Number of Miles from Calcutta.	Time of Transit from Station to Station.	Fare. 1st Class.* R.	A.	P.
		h. m.	R.	A.	P.
Howrah (*terminus*)	1	......	0	1	0
Bally...	6	......	0	10	6
Connaghur	9	......	0	15	0
Serampore	13	0·30	1	3	6
Biddabatty	16	......	1	8	0
Chandernagore ...	21	0·21	1	15	6
Hooghly	24	......	2	4	0
Mugrah	30	......	2	13	0
Pundoosh	38	......	3	10	6
Boinchee	44	......	4	3	6
Mymarree	51	......	4	14	0
Suktikur	60	......	5	10	0
Burdwan	67	1·54	6	6	0
Mankoor†	90	......	8	8	6
Pannaghur	97	......	9	3	0
Raneegunj ...	121	2·5	11	7	0
Assensore	10	......	0	15	0
Seetarampore ...	16	......	1	8	0
Burrakur	22	......	2	1	0
Gooshkarrah	87	......	8	4	0
Beddish	94	......	8	14	6
Bulpoor	99	......	9	4	6
Ahmoodpore	111	......	10	6	6
Synthees	119	......	11	4	0
Mullarpoor	124	......	12	1	6
Rampore Haut ...	136	2·59	12	13	6
Nulhatee	145	......	13	11	0
Moorarooe	155	......	14	10	0
Pakowr	169	......	15	15	0
Bahawa	185	......	17	7	0
Teen Pahar	196	......	18	6	0
Rajmahal† ...	203	3·6	19	0	6
Maharajpore ...	209	......	19	9	6
Sahibgunj	220	5·7	20	10	0
Peerpyntee	234	......	21	15	0
Colgong	248	......	23	1	0
Ghogah	252	......	23	10	0
Bhaugulpore	265	......	24	13	6
Sultangunj	279	......	26	2	6

Name of Station.	Number of Miles from Calcutta.	Time of Transit from Station to Station.	Fare. 1st Class.* R.	A.	P.
		h. m.	R.	A.	P.
Burriarpore	290	......	27	3	0
Jumalpore	298	3·20	27	15	0
Monghyr†	303	0·40	28	6	6
Durrarah	305	......	0	12	0
Kujrah	316	......	1	12	6
Luckeeserai	327	......	2	11	6
Burhea	336	......	3	9	0
Mokameh	347	......	4	9	6
Barrh	363	......	6	3	0
Bucktearpore ...	374	......	7	3	6
Futwah	389	......	8	8	6
Patna	396	......	9	4	6
Bankipore	402	......	9	13	6
Dinapore	408	4·56	10	6	6
Bihta	419	......	11	7	0
Arrah	433	......	12	10	6
Beehea	446	......	13	15	6
Rogonathpore ...	455	......	14	13	0
Doomraon	465	......	15	12	0
Buxar	476	2·50	16	11	0
Gubmer	488	......	17	14	6
Dildarnuggur ...	498	......	18	13	6
Zumaneah	506	......	19	9	6
Sukuldeah	523	......	21	1	6
Mogul Serai ...	534	2 24	22	3	6
Benares†	540	0·15	22	12	6
Ahrowra Road ...	543	......	22	15	6
Chunar	554	......	24	1	6
Puharree	564	...	24	15	0
Mirzapore	573	1·41	25	14	0
Guepoora	585	......	27	0	0
Nuwaee	595	......	27	13	6
Sirsa Road	605	......	28	14	0
Kurchuna	618	......	30	0	0
Jumna Station	626	2·15			
Allahabad	630	......	59	14	6
Cawnpore	749	5·20	70	15	6
Agra	905	7·40	85	11	0
Delhi	1019	5·28	96	3	9

Or: Calcutta to Allahabad, 32*h*. 40 *m*. Allahabad to Delhi, 13*h*. 13*m*. Total hours from Calcutta to Delhi, 51*h*. 20*m*

* The 2nd Class fares are exactly half those of the 1st.

† Stations *indented* are branch lines.